The Open University
Arts: A Third Level Course
The Rise of Modernism in Music 1890–1935
Units 22–24

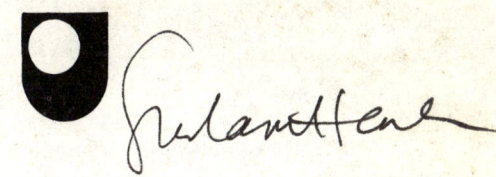

IVES AND VARÈSE

Prepared for the Course Team by Ian Bonighton
and Richard Middleton

The Open University Press

The Open University Press
Walton Hall, Milton Keynes
MK7 6AA

First published 1979

Designed by the Media Development Group of the Open University.

Printed photolitho in Great Britain by
Ebenezer Baylis & Son Limited,
Leicester and London

ISBN 0 335 05456 0

This text forms part of an Open University course. The complete list of units in the course
appears at the end of this text.

For general availability of supporting material referred to in this text, please write to
Open University Educational Enterprises Limited, 12 Cofferidge Close, Stony Stratford,
Milton Keynes, MK11 1BY, Great Britain.

Further information on Open University courses may be obtained from the Admissions
Office, The Open University, P.O. Box 48, Walton Hall, Milton Keynes, MK7 6AB.

1.1

Contents

Introduction

American music as a topic is both large and relatively neglected. Since it 'comes of age' in the twentieth century, it is an essential component of a course on the 'rise of modernism'; and yet limitations of time and space mean that we must single out just a few of the significant trends. The music of Charles Ives and Edgard Varèse represents some of the most important developments, and a further strand, early jazz, is covered in the next block. Particularly in the 1920s modern music in the USA was very lively, and it would be profitable to supplement these units by consulting books listed in the bibliography (p. 106) for information on such figures as Aaron Copland, Henry Cowell and George Gershwin.

This block introduces the music of Ives and Varèse and puts it into context, both the context of other American music of the time and of contemporary European music. TV programme 3 provides relevant background material, particularly on Ives, and there are two associated radio programmes: Radio programme 12 is a study of Ives' Fourth Symphony and is meant to be used in conjunction with Section 6 of these units; Radio programme 15 discusses Varèse and includes an analysis of *Density 21.5*, which is connected with Section 12. For this block you will need Records 8 and 9, *Scores 7* and also the score of Ives' *Concord* Sonata which you are required to buy.

The first draft of these units was prepared by the late Ian Bonighton. I have revised this and added some new material. Sections 1, 8, 10, 11, 13 and 14 are entirely mine. I hope Dr Bonighton would not be too unhappy with the final shape of the units, and I would like them to stand as a memorial to him.

Richard Middleton

1 Some American background

The essential nature of what a specifically American music would be like was succinctly described in 1770 by a Boston tanner turned composer called William Billings (1746–1800). 'I think it best,' he wrote, 'for every Composer to be his own Carver'. The rough, vigorous songs, hymns and 'fuging tunes' of Billings and other members of the so-called First New England School live up to this prescription. Over a hundred years later Billings' impatient attitude to musical conventions would be echoed by Charles Ives. By then, however, the musical scene was very different. The indigenous eighteenth-century New England style had long disintegrated. The unity of sacred and secular, 'cultivated' and 'vernacular' had been split. Increasing urbanization in the east of the country led to a growing taste for 'cultivated' European music; at that time this meant German music above all. An influx of German teachers and performers established themselves, and before long the focus of every American composer's ambitions lay in Germany. Meanwhile 'vernacular' music — folksong and dance, spirituals and gospel hymns, minstrel song, wind band music, ragtime — developed strong traditions; but in the world of genteel parlour song and piano music, light opera and orchestral music these traditions were either unknown or regarded with contempt.

By the late nineteenth century new institutions like the New England Conservatory in Boston, august periodicals such as *Dwight's Journal*, newly established orchestras (New York Philharmonic 1842, Boston Symphony 1881) and a new generation of composers — notably the Second New England School of John Knowles Paine (1839–1906), George Chadwick (1854–1931), Horatio Parker (1863–1919) and others — were solidifying what Ives called the 'German rule'. The Second New England School, broadly speaking, followed the 'classicistic' nineteenth-century German tradition (Mendelssohn, Brahms, etc.); Edward MacDowell (1861–1908) offered a more picturesque romantic style. But there was very little one could call 'American'. Ordinary Americans commonly regarded the world of 'cultivated' music-making as 'useless' and effete. 'Thus crystallized an American view of fine-art music as essentially the province of females, foreigners, or effeminates . . .'[1]

The first substantial signs of change appear in the early years of the twentieth century. Charles T. Griffes (1884–1921) abandoned German influence for that of Debussy, Scriabin, Stravinsky and oriental music, but died before fulfilling his promise. Henry Gilbert (1868–1928) and Arthur Farwell (1872–1951) tried to incorporate elements of indigenous American musics — black music and Indian music respectively — into their works. Nationalistic feelings, often connected with interest in folk music, began to appear. Still, however, such men worked in an almost total vacuum. There was virtually no audience for modern music in America; the growth of an avant-garde movement in music lagged behind similar developments in the other arts. As Aaron Copland later wrote, 'Contemporary music as an organized movement in the USA was born at the end of the First World War.'[2] When European modernists crossed the Atlantic, either to visit or, like Edgard Varèse, to stay (he came in 1915), they found a substantial task of propaganda and dissemination ahead of them and their American colleagues.

1 Wiley Hitchcock, *Music in the United States: A Historical Introduction*, Prentice-Hall 1969, p. 53.

2 Aaron Copland, *Our New Music*, McGraw-Hill 1941, p. 137.

PART 1: IVES

2 Biographical details

2.1 Childhood

Charles Edward Ives was born on 20 October 1874 in Danbury, Connecticut, where his father George E. Ives was a musician and teacher. The influence of this man on his son was enormous and must have started very soon after Charles' birth. Writing in 1930 Ives said of his father:

> [He] was a musician and teacher (in Danbury and neighbouring villages) of the violin, piano (brass and woodwind instruments), harmony, sight reading, (and ear training), etc. He played in and taught the brass band (and orchestra), led the church choirs, the music at the Camp Meetings, and the local Choral Society. He had a reverence, a devotion, and a talent for music which was unusual. His interest lay not only in what had been done but in what might be done . . . He started all the children of the family — and most of the children of the town for that matter — on Bach and Stephen Foster. (Quite shortly after they were born — always regardless of whether they had, would have, or wouldn't have any musical gifts or sense, etc. —) . . . [1]

Under the guidance of such a man, and in a family environment which treated musical activity as a normal part of everyday life, it seemed inevitable that Ives should receive a unique, yet thorough training. This training, however, was not limited to the study of the basic skills of the musical craft; George Ives had a scientific interest in the physics of music and 'his study of acoustics led him to many experiments into the character of musical instruments and tonal combinations, and even into the division of the tone,'[2] and this information and spirit of inquiry was also passed on to his son.

Formal music lessons began when Ives was five years old and continued until his father's death in 1894. These included instruction in piano, violin and cornet playing, together with a study of harmony and counterpoint (from the works of Bach) and musical history. Practical experience was gained by playing in the town band, usually on one of the drums, and this led to some of Ives' earliest musical experiments. At the request of the neighbours the drum parts were practised on the piano, but the constant repetition of the same set of notes proved too monotonous for an enthusiastic boy. Instead, Ives began to experiment with groups of notes in an attempt to imitate the sounds of the various drums — closely grouped notes in the right hand for the snare drum and wider-spaced chords in the bass to represent the bass drum, while explosive or heavy accents were often played with the fist or the flat of the hand.

Later in his life Ives commented on this practice: 'I remember distinctly, after this habit became a matter of years, that going back to the usual consonant triads, chords, etc., something strong seemed more or less missing (at least quite often, if not always) . . .'[3] and he was to use this cluster technique in many of his mature works.

By the time he was nine or ten years old Ives was expected to be able to sing the tune of a song in one key while the accompaniment was played in another totally unrelated key, in order to 'stretch' his ears and mind. Such polytonal experiments had to be taken seriously and there were severe consequences for the boy who regarded it as a

---

1 Letter to John Tasker Howard, 30 June 1930. Quoted in Charles E. Ives, *Memos*, John Kirkpatrick (ed.), Calder & Boyars 1972, pp. 236–37. (Hereafter referred to as *Memos*.)
2 *Memos*, p. 237.
3 *Memos*, p. 43.

George E. Ives in his bandmaster's uniform, c. 1890

thoughtless prank. '. . . Father was not against a reasonable amount of "boy's fooling"
. . . as playing left hand accompaniments in one key and tune in right hand in another
. . . He made us stick to the end, not stop when it got hard. This led into trying to
write duets and pieces in more than one key, or two keys together . . .'[1] As with the
drum experiments, these early polytonal experiences were to form an important basis
for many of Ives' mature compositions.

A third interest stimulated during this early period of training came from some of
George Ives' experiments. Many of these led his fellow townsmen to describe him as a
'crank', but the experiments were carried out with a surprising degree of thoroughness
and not a little ingenuity; they were often concerned with a subject that was to exercise
many minds in the 1930s and 40s — the subdivision of the octave into units smaller than
the semitone. Some of the experiments were carried out with conventional instruments
such as the slide cornet which, with its ability to lengthen or shorten the sounding
length of the pipe, was a logical choice. Others were carried out with conventional
instruments that had been modified in some way to accommodate the new tuning
system; a piano tuned to the actual harmonic series of its lowest note was one such
experimental device. A third group of experiments was carried out on specially constructed instruments ranging from collections of tuned glasses for very small intervals
to a set of twenty-four or more violin strings stretched over a clothes press and held

1 *Memos*, p. 46.

8

down with weights. George Ives would play quarter-tone melodies on this instrument and try to get the family to sing them, but this latter part of the experiment was soon abandoned except as a means of punishment.

The results of these experiments left a profound impression on the young Ives and later in his life he was to write a fairly lengthy article on the subject of quarter-tone music (published in the *Franco-American Music Society Bulletin* of 25 March 1925) and to make considerable use of these intervals in his string writing, as we shall see when we come to examine sections of the Fourth Symphony.

However, all this experimental thinking was well balanced in Ives' musical education by a thorough study of conventional musical procedures, for George Ives believed that it was necessary to be able to do a thing the 'right' (or conventional) way properly before attempting to do it the unconventional (or 'wrong') way. As a result of this he continued to teach his son harmony and counterpoint from the works of Bach. When Charles began his musical studies at Yale he felt that he had already covered the required syllabus in this field under his father's guidance.

EXERCISE

In what specific 'modernist' techniques might Charles Ives have first acquired an interest through experiments dating from his childhood?

DISCUSSION

1 Clusters
2 Polytonality
3 Quarter tones

2.2   The church organist

The colonists of New England had been fiercely devout men and women who regarded the singing of psalms as an integral part of life. They produced many composers and musicians who provided a considerable number of anthems, hymns, psalm tunes and assorted patriotic pieces, most notably those in the vigorous, rough-hewn style of the First New England School. However, these men waned in popularity in the late eighteenth and early nineteenth centuries, and their music was replaced by the more genteel hymns of men like Lowell Mason (1792–1872), the (largely anonymous) camp-meeting hymns produced for the religious revivals of the early nineteenth century and, in the second half of the century, the hymns of city revivalist campaigns written by such composers as Ira D. Sankey (1840–1908).

As a direct result of the labours of itinerant preachers or circuit riders who travelled the countryside with their prayers, sermons and hymns, the camp meeting emerged as a recognized form of religious experience. No matter how far or how fast a circuit rider travelled he could not hope to reach all the population within his chosen district, so it was only natural that, as the result of advance publicity, people from a large area should converge at a specified place to hear his words and to participate in the meeting. Since many of these rural workers and their families had to travel vast distances to attend they usually came prepared to stay for several days and arrived equipped with bedding and food for their stay. The numbers at any one meeting have been variously estimated as ranging from 2,000 to 20,000; but whatever the truth we may be certain that the attendances were large. The singing of hymns and spiritual songs by these vast numbers was an important part of the meetings and often went on through the night.

In his *Memos* Ives gives us a vivid picture of his father leading such a meeting in their hymns:

> I remember, when I was a boy—at the outdoor Camp Meeting services in Redding, all the farmers, their families and field hands, for miles around, would come afoot or in their wagons . . . Father, who led the singing, sometimes with his cornet or his voice, sometimes with both voice and arms, and sometimes in the quieter hymns with a French horn or violin, would always encourage the people to sing their own way. [1]

The city revivalist campaigns also gave rise to a renewed interest in hymn singing and men like Lowell Mason, composer of some 1,200 original hymn tunes and adaptor of nearly 500 melodies by other composers, and Ira Sankey (responsible for six volumes of *Gospel Hymns* published between 1875 and 1894) became extremely influential in the field of religious music.

In such an atmosphere it is not at all surprising that Charles Ives became a church organist. What is surprising is the fact that he was considered sufficiently accomplished to accept the post of organist at the Second Congregational Church in Danbury in February 1889 at the age of fourteen. He remained there until 1892 when he was appointed organist at St Thomas Church, New Haven, Connecticutt (1892–94) and then continued his career at the First Presbyterian Church, Bloomfield, New Jersey (1899), and the Central Presbyterian Church, 57th Street, New York (1899–1902). Naturally this thirteen-year period of regular musical employment left a permanent mark on Ives' musical thinking.

Such a long exposure to (and familiarity with) protestant hymnology had two quite opposite effects: on the one hand it laid the foundations for a lifelong love of certain well-known hymn tunes (including *Beulah Land, Woodworth, Nearer My God to Thee, Nettleton* and the like) and on the other it led to an intense dislike of the harmonic treatment generally given to these melodies. Remembering the full-bodied (and often original) style of singing at the camp meetings, Ives commented:

> I've heard the same hymns played by nice celebrated organists and sung by highly-known singers in beautifully upholstered churches, and in the process everything in the music was emasculated . . . They take a mountain and make a sponge cake of it . . . [2]

His own harmonization often contained bolder strokes more worthy of a man who could easily play a hymn tune in one key and its accompaniment in another. Naturally, congregations complained of his treatment at times, but some of his musical friends stood by him. Ives found the simple harmonies in the hymnal monotonous and childish, and how could God be pleased with music that men could not stand?

Despite the monotony of hymn playing, the post of organist held certain advantages. One of these was the opportunity it gave Ives to play his own works as it was largely by playing and constant revision that he was able to clarify his ideas. Many of his important works began in this way; his Third Symphony, for example, started life as a series of organ pieces. Two of the movements were orchestrated revisions of organ works written around 1901 and the last movement was originally an organ prelude on the hymn tune *Woodworth*.

There were, however, certain compromises to be made in return for this privilege.

> And in playing them at a service, is one justified in doing something which, to him, is quite in keeping with his understanding and feelings—but [not] to the

1 *Memos*, pp. 132–33.
2 *Memos*, p. 133.

congregation, who [may be] unused to the idiom, or rather some of the sound combinations, and so naturally might misunderstand and be disturbed? The Third String Quartet (not finished I think for this reason) and the Third Symphony especially were to some extent boiled down, or rather suppressed, technically speaking.[1]

In other words, the audience does deserve some consideration; certainly some concesssion should be made, in Ives' opinion, for people who have come together for worship and for whom the music is an incidental thing. A congregation has certain rights—unlike a concert audience or a personal friend they cannot just get up and walk out if they are dissatisfied. It is perhaps for this reason that Ives felt that he was only able to do justice to religious themes when he knew that they would be played in a secular context. The last movement of the Fourth Symphony, the second movement of the First String Quartet, the last movement of the Second Orchestral Set, the already mentioned Third Symphony and parts of the violin sonatas are only a few of the works based on religious themes, and these show a greater freedom and a more imaginative treatment than the music written specifically for church use.

2.3   The undergraduate

Ives had attended the Danbury Academy and then the Danbury High School for his general education. However, in 1893 he entered the Hopkins Grammar School, New Haven, to prepare him for admission to Yale University where he was duly enrolled the following year. His course of study was at first a general education and Ives studied the usual curriculum which included Greek, Latin, French, German, English Literature, Mathematics, Political Science and Philosophy. In his third and fourth years he was officially able to include a number of music subjects (such as counterpoint, instrumentation and composition) although it is certain that in his first two years Ives attended many of the music lectures offered, as an auditor rather than as a participant.

The head of the music faculty at that time was Professor Horatio Parker, a composer considered by his contemporaries to be one of the greatest men in American music. He had originally studied in Germany under Rheinberger and one of his early appointments had been to a conservatorium under the direction of Dvořák, who had made a lasting impression on the young Parker. His appointment at Yale raised that post to new importance, his ability being highly respected in the fields of composition, conducting and teaching.

Later in his life Ives was to comment favourably on Parker's works, remarking on the dignity and depth of his choral music despite the fact that he felt it to be too bound up with the 'German rule' of the textbooks. The fact that this music was seldom of a trivial nature led Ives to hold—at least in retrospect—a certain degree of respect for his teacher. However, things were very different at the start of their relationship. As already noted, Ives had been thoroughly instructed in harmony and counterpoint at an early age by his father; now, when Parker took him over the same ground (using identical textbooks and exercises in some cases) he found the revision boring, despite the fact that a somewhat higher standard was expected.

Friction was also generated over the subject of composition:

> In the beginning of Freshman year, and getting assigned to classes, Parker asked me to bring him whatever manuscripts I had written. Among them, a song, *At Parting*—in it, some unresolved dissonances, one ending on a [high] E flat [in the] key [of] G major, and stops there unresolved. Parker said, 'There's no excuse for that—an E flat way up there and stopping, and the nearest D natural way down two octaves.'—etc.[2]

1   *Memos*, p. 128.
2   *Memos*, p. 116.

Fortunately Parker took most of Ives' compositions in the spirit of a joke and experimental ideas were not so much suppressed as ignored. Fortunately, also, Ives continued to write in his own highly individual style, preferring to the ideas of Parker the training given to him by his father, who was not a composer and certainly very little known.

While the peace of the classroom was on the whole being maintained by regular application to class exercises, Ives was occasionally trying out some of his own music, not only in the organ works he was playing on Sundays, but also with the orchestra of the Hyperion Theatre in New Haven. The leader of this group was a friend and allowed him to conduct some of his short pieces. In addition he wrote music for student entertainments and revues, and he would often stand in briefly for the regular pianist at a New Haven vaudeville theatre (and later silent cinema) called Poli's: on these occasions he was remembered as playing dissonant 'raggy' off-beat and polytonal music, and some of this went into later compositions, especially ragtime-influenced pieces. [1]

The First Symphony was written while Ives was still a student at Yale, and was shown to Parker who objected violently since the first subject modulated through some six or eight keys while supposed to be in D minor. He strongly suggested that Ives should write another first movement, but the composer's insistence was such that Parker relented.

> He smiled and let me do it, saying 'But you must promise to end in D minor.' And also he didn't like the original slow movement, as it started on G flat — he said it should start in F. Near the end 'the boys got going' — so at the request of Parker . . . I wrote a nice formal one — but the first is better! [2]

Also written at this time was a *Prelude and Postlude for a Thanksgiving Service*, to be played on the organ of the Center Church, New Haven, on Thanksgiving Day 1897. Ives later described this as 'the first piece that seems to me to be much good or any good now'.

> The *Postlude* started with a C minor chord with a D minor chord over it, together, and later major and minor chords together, a tone apart. This was to represent the sternness and strength and austerity of the Puritan character, and it seemed to me that any of the major, minor or diminished chords used alone gave too much a feeling of bodily ease, which the Puritans did not give in to. There is also in this some free counterpoint in different keys, and two rhythms going together. There is a scythe or reaping Harvest Theme, which is a kind of off-beat, off-key counterpoint. Six or eight years later . . . these two pieces were arranged as a single movement for orchestra in the shape now found . . . [3]

This finished version of the *Prelude and Postlude* may be heard as the 'Thanksgiving' movement from the *Holidays* Symphony. Even today this music has a strangely disconcerting effect on many people; it is no wonder that 'Parker made some funny cracks about it' when we consider the effect it must have had on a nineteenth-century German-trained academic with very distinct ideas about the sort of music that was appropriate to a church or a symphony.

EXERCISE

From what you know of Ives' time at Yale, say what aspects of his personality this period demonstrates.

---

1 See *Memos*, pp. 56–57.
2 *Memos*, p. 51.
3 *Memos*, p. 39

DISCUSSION

1 Eclecticism — church music, theatre music, entertainment, symphony.
2 Integrity and stubbornness — he refused to conform to Parker's precepts.
3 An idealistic belief in the seriousness of music — his tribute to Parker's own music shows this.

2.4 The 'part-time composer'

After his graduation from Yale in 1898 Ives was faced with a problem familiar to many young undergraduates — how to make a living. Naturally there was a strong temptation to undertake a musical career but this was swiftly squashed, for Ives was too well aware that any composer, no matter how good, would have trouble providing for a wife and family. Although he was not to marry for another eight years he took all these things into account when making the important decision to abandon the professional stand and become a 'weekend composer'. In his *Memos* Ives recounts the logic which led him to accept this position without complaint.

> Father felt that a man could keep his music-interest stronger, cleaner, bigger and freer if he didn't try to make a living out of it. Assuming a man lived by himself and with no dependents, no one to feed but himself, and willing to live as simply as Thoreau — [he] might write music that no one would play, publish, listen to, or buy. *But* — if he has a nice wife, and some nice children, how can he let the children starve on his dissonances — answer that, Eddy! So he has to weaken (and as a man he should weaken for his children), but his music (some of it) more than weakens — it goes 'ta ta' for money — bad for him, bad for music, but good for his boys!![1]

The decision to sentence himself to long hours of labour after a normal working day rather than make compromises in his compositional style must have been a hard one to make, but it still did nothing to help Ives to decide on a distinct career. Perhaps his decision to enter the world of insurance was due to his feeling that '. . . to be thrown with people of all conditions all day long, for a good part of a man's life, widens rather than cramps his sensibilities'[2] or perhaps it was (as Henry and Sidney Cowell suggest) that

> His life work must fulfill his highest ideals by giving him the best possible opportunity to do the most good for the largest number of people. And it must be the kind of activity that had room at the top for men of originality, something with enough variety and scope for a man to get his teeth into and make himself felt.

> To Ives it seemed obvious that the business of life insurance perfectly met these requirements. In 1898 . . . most people in the United States had been thoroughly convinced that the insurance companies were disinterested benefactors of the common man. So not long after Ivy Day, Ives went to New York to begin the 'practice of life insurance' much as his classmates went into medicine or the ministry.[3]

Ives' first post was with the Mutual Life Insurance Company, and on his salary of $5 a week he joined with several friends to rent an apartment (promptly renamed 'Poverty Flat') in New York. In the spring of 1899 he was transferred to the Raymond Agency who were general agents for his firm and it was here that he met Julian Myrick. This

1 *Memos*, p. 131.
2 *Memos*, p. 131.
3 Henry and Sidney Cowell, *Charles Ives and His Music*, Oxford University Press 1955, p. 38.

friendship was to be the real start of their business careers, for in January 1907 Ives and Myrick formed a partnership and secured a general agency with the Washington Life Insurance Company of New York. In 1908, however, the parent company sold its stock to another firm which cancelled the Ives and Myrick general agency, but the potential disaster was averted by the Mutual Life Insurance Company, Ives' previous employers, who made it clear that the general efficiency and ability of the new partnership had attracted their attention.

The business partnership lasted until Ives retired in 1930 because of ill health. As a sideline it is of interest to note that Julian Myrick celebrated his fiftieth year in the insurance world in 1949 as Vice President and General Manager of the Mutual Life Insurance Company of New York.

The decision not to compromise his musical style placed Ives in a very awkward position as a composer. Certainly he was able to write as he wished, without having to 'conform' to what he often criticized as the 'rules of harmony', but the price for this freedom was high—he was obliged to work long and unsocial hours and had to survive without the usual stimuli of performances, concerts and contact with fellow composers. During this period very few of his works received performances other than private rehearsals and run-throughs, and the reaction to these, when professional players were involved, was usually one of mirth or incredulity. These facts contributed almost as much to his highly individual style of writing as did his early training and his father's musical experiments.

Charles Ives at Battery Park, c. 1913

Although Ives still occasionally found time to attend concerts and performances of the works of his favourite composers the pleasure that he gained from such events was often limited.

> I find that most musicians, critics, etc., take it for granted that a man who composes music must, as a result, be conversant with all the music that has been written in the world up to last night. So many apparently seem surprised, and can't understand why I don't know this piece or that piece of this composer or that composer . . .

> As I see it, there are only about two reasons why I don't. One is that, being in business for so many years, I had only evenings, Saturday afternoons and Sundays, and summer vacations of two or three weeks, in which to work. For this reason . . . I got out of the habit of going to concerts, especially in the evenings. I always seemed to have something I was working on, and it was this, and the fact that my time was limited, that kept me from going out much.[1]

However, the time factor was not the only thing that limited the pleasure of concert going. Much of Ives' work was done in his head before being committed to paper, and the process of actively listening to any other music was a distraction.

> . . . on account of having only a limited time in which to work, I got into the habit of carrying things in my mind which were not put down, or only partly put down, on paper. As this was the case most of the time, I found that listening to music (especially if in the programs there were things with which I was not familiar) tended to throw me out of my stride. I'll admit it may have been a kind of weakness on my part, but I found that listening to concert music seemed to confuse me in my own work, maybe not to a great extent, but enough to throw me off somewhat from what I had in mind or purposed.[2]

Ives continued writing in these circumstances until interrupted by ill health. The extra work imposed by the problems of the First World War (Ives was working to raise money for Red Cross and Liberty Loan drives) not only prevented him from continuing with his compositional activities but also caused a serious physical break-down. In 1918 he was forced to rest for six months by an illness which left him with permanent cardiac damage and largely as a result of this period of thinking and reflecting Ives decided early in the following year that the works he had written should be put at the disposal of the general public.

He therefore had the *Concord* Sonata, together with the volume of *Essays Before a Sonata* and a collection of *114 Songs*, privately printed and distributed without copyright. By so doing Ives hoped to bypass the hard-bitten professional musicians who had so often criticized his music as too difficult to play and the academics who were horrified at the innovatory nature of his work. He hoped instead to appeal directly to 'the average person able to tinker a little at the keyboard'. Why he chose this course will never be known, but the results were predictable: works such as the *Concord* Sonata are, even today, regarded by professional performers as massive undertakings, yet Ives was suggesting that this work might be of interest to the average pianist and hoping that some of his fiendishly difficult songs would be sung by amateurs for pleasure.

Perhaps Ives was over-estimating the abilities of 'the average person'; his political philosophy, an idealistic belief in the Common Man and the Majority Mind, often led

---

1 *Memos*, pp. 136–37.
2 *Memos*, p. 137.

him to do this. Perhaps he was simply using his own abilities as a yardstick, for in later years he wrote in his *Memos*:

> . . . with one or two exceptions there are no songs in my book of *114 Songs* which I haven't sung and couldn't sing, especially when I was writing them. I will admit that, if I haven't seen them for some time, as is the case with many of them, it takes a little practice and effort to get them back in the ears and mind. But there are but few of the songs that I can't (after a few hours of renewing acquaintance) sing, although I don't want to infer here that I am a singer. I have a rough voice, but I can make a noise on the right note at the right time and on the right interval—and, in spite of the piano, get the song going somewhere. Any singer can do the same thing if he makes up his mind to it, unless he is a congenital musical defective, or with about the same musical mentality that is sometimes the possession of famous operatic stars.
>
> There is nothing that I have ever written for a piano that I haven't been able to play. Give me a day or so (but sometimes a year or two too) of practice and I can always get the music back into my fingers. Not that I can play as well as I'd like to, but at least I can convince myself that it's playable. [1]

Ives wrote almost no music after 1920. This can be explained perhaps as the effect of the mirth that the publication of the *Concord* Sonata and the *Songs* aroused in many musical circles and the amount of time taken up by their preparation and publication. Probably also ill health, exhaustion and depression at the nature of political and social developments in the twenties had something to do with it. He began a number of sketches (nearly all of which were left unfinished) and did a considerable amount of literary work, largely of a political nature, but composition was apparently a thing of the past. Around the end of 1926, as his wife recalled, 'he came downstairs one day with tears in his eyes, and said he couldn't seem to compose any more—nothing went well, nothing sounded right' [2].

On 1 January 1930 Ives retired from business, but despite this change the remainder of his life was marred by continued ill health. In 1932–33 he travelled through Europe, visiting France, Germany, Switzerland, Italy and England on an extended holiday and he returned once again to England in 1934. Now, however, Ives was beginning to suffer from cataracts in both eyes so he returned to New York to edit and supervise the copying of a number of his works. This task, together with the compilation of his *Memos* ('not memoirs—no one but the President of a nice Bank or Golf Club, or a dead Prime Minister, can write memoirs'), occupied him throughout the remainder of his life, and although he did not die until 19 May 1954 he wrote no new music.

EXERCISE

Why do you think Ives continued to write in his own personal style (so often described as 'dissonant', 'off-beat', 'off-key' or 'polytonal'), particularly when a composer such as Parker had advised him to reconsider his ideas?

DISCUSSION

Ives' early training had taught him the value of experiment. His father's experiments had demonstrated to him that there were other pleasing sounds than those generally accepted or taught as 'correct' and this demonstration had taken the form of practical tests rather than a collection of textbook quotations or 'rules'. A successful composer

1   *Memos*, p. 142.
2   *Memos*, p. 279.

Charles Ives in 1947, photograph by Frank Gerrantana   *Charles and Harmony Ives at their West Redding home in late 1920s*

must be a creator—a maker of things that have not been before, rather than a manufacturer who concocts works according to a pattern or a set of rules, and as such he must learn to rely on experimental evidence.

Also, Ives was writing the way he did from choice and not from the necessity brought about by a lack of knowledge of alternative styles. He had inspected a wide range of the musical materials available to him (in his early training under his father's guidance), selected several, tested these (in his period as an organist and composer of church music) and finally settled for one particular approach. Parker, on the other hand, was suggesting that Ives should take over a ready-made system of harmonies, melodic formulas and rhythmic patterns, all of which were already well established musical features (and therefore potentially 'worked out' from the creator's point of view) and all of which had been reduced by theorists to a set of 'rules' or procedures which would only allow imitation. Finally, these 'recipes' were taught by quotation rather than demonstration and the very practical reasons for which these procedures had been introduced were often no longer valid, or else forgotten.

Ives' comments:

> I am fully convinced [that], if music be not allowed to grow, if it's denied the privilege of evolution that all other arts and life have, if [in the] natural processes of ear and mind it is not allowed to grow bigger by finding possibilities that nature has for music, more and wider scales, new combinations of tone, new keys and more keys and beats, and phrases together—if it just sticks (as it does today) to one key, one single and easy rhythm, and the rules made to boss them—then music, before many years, cannot be composed—everything will be used up—endless repetitions of static melodies, harmonies, resolutions and

17

meters—and music as a creative art will die—for to compose will be but to manufacture conventionalized MUSH—and that's about what student composers are being taught to do.[1]

Any art or any habit of life, if it is limited chronically to a few processes that are the easiest to acquire (and for that reason are said to be some natural laws), must at some time, quite probably, become so weakened that it is neither a part of art nor a part of life. Consonance is a relative thing (just a nice name for a nice habit). It is a natural enough part of music, but not the whole, or the only one. The simplest ratios, often called perfect consonances, have been used so long and so constantly that not only music, but musicians and audiences, have become more or less soft. If they hear anything but doh-me-soh or a near cousin, they have to be carried out on a stretcher.[2]

1 *Memos*, p. 48.
2 *Memos*, p. 42.

3 Some technical details

Having seen what may be described as the 'breeding ground' for the experimental aspects of Ives' musical style, let us now examine some of the techniques that made his style so individual. You will find that in some cases there are parallels with the music you have already studied by Ives' European contemporaries. For a long time much of the 'case for Ives' was put in terms of the supposed fact that he anticipated many of the innovations of the European modernists (as indeed he did). However, the musical results in Ives' case are very different. When early performances led to the assumption by critics that he had been *influenced* by the Europeans, he wrote,

> All the music that I have written, with the exception of a dozen or fifteen songs, was completed before I had seen or heard any of the music of the European composers . . . It is interesting . . . to know . . . that I . . . have been influenced by . . . Hindemith . . . who didn't really start to compose until about 1920 . . . several years after I had completed all of my . . . music . . . which . . . [supposedly] is influenced by Hindemith . . .[1]

Ives' studio

In the same letter Ives declared he had not up to that time (1931) heard nor seen any of Schoenberg's music. Elsewhere he wrote:

> I've never heard or seen the score of the *Sacre du Printemps* . . . *Putnam's Camp* . . . [supposedly] . . . influenced by the *Sacre du Printemps* . . . [was] written before Stravinsky wrote the *Sacre* . . . Personally I don't think they have anything in common. It wasn't until about 1919 or 20 that I first heard any of Stravinsky's music.[2]

3.1 The use of clusters

A cluster is simply a group of adjacent (or near adjacent) notes played simultaneously in chordal form. Thus a hand placed on a piano keyboard to cover an adjoining series

1 Letter to the pianist E. Robert Schmitz, quoted in *Memos*, pp. 27–28.
2 *Memos*, p. 138.

of black and white notes would be a cluster, as would a hand (or arm) covering only an adjacent group of black or white notes.

chromatic cluster   white-note cluster   black-note cluster

Ives' use of this type of chordal construction could have originated in one of several ways. In the first place, it may have been the result of polytonal thinking: a combination of the keys of C major and F sharp major, for example, would produce a number of such clusters, as would any grouping of two keys a semitone apart (such as C major and C sharp major played simultaneously). It is, however, more likely that the use of the cluster was suggested by other means, and one of these possible sources is Ives' desire to make music more expressive. We have already seen how, in his *Prelude and Postlude for a Thanksgiving Service*, he superimposed the chords of C minor and D minor (making a cluster of the notes C, D, E flat, F, G and A) and later used 'major and minor chords together a tone apart' in order to express 'the sternness and strength and austerity of the Puritan character'.

Another possible source may be found within the tonal system itself. The basic practice of making chords by the superimposition of notes a third apart can be logically extended by the addition of further thirds above the basic triad. One such chord would be C, E, G, B, D, F and A. If the notes of this chord are rearranged (or, technically speaking, put into another inversion), it is easy to arrive at such a complex as A, B, C, D, E, F, G—a white-note cluster. Other chords when extended could provide black-note clusters (such as D, F sharp, A sharp, C sharp, E and G sharp rearranged to form F sharp, G sharp, A sharp and C sharp) or chromatic clusters (formed by chords such as C, E flat, G, B, D, F, A, C sharp, E, which would allow the extraction of C, C sharp, D, E flat, E natural and F).

However, regardless of the system employed to generate these clusters, the fact is that Ives used them with a regularity that has made them an essential part of his musical style. Here are a few short examples:

1 Superimposition of chords—potential clusters—from the song 'Paracelsus'. The wide distance between the chords, however, ensures that the dissonant element is minimized.

2 A compilation of thirds. Again, the potentially dissonant notes are well separated. From 'Majority' (*Scores 7*, p. 9 last bar)

3 Another example from 'Paracelsus'. This time the cluster (a white-note cluster) is closely spaced and is made up of two superimposed chords, each built of thirds.

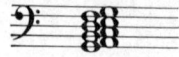

Ives uses these clusters for a variety of purposes. Melodically they are often employed to 'thicken' or reinforce a melodic line to ensure that it stands out clearly from the remainder of the musical texture. Where other composers in the past had done this by doubling the melody at the octave, the third or the sixth, Ives prefers to use the closer cluster which has no tonal connotations and therefore will not interfere with the supporting chord progression. In other words, the cluster is, in this case, used for colouristic purposes to make the listener's task of separating information from support a simpler one.

Harmonically the cluster may be (as we have seen) nothing more than a complex chord which has been somewhat telescoped to leave only the adjacent notes. On the other hand, however, it may be used as a means of building and releasing harmonic tension within a work. In this latter case the process is simplified by the use of various types of cluster: a gradual change from a situation such as that shown above in example 1 to a closer (and therefore more dissonant) cluster — as shown in example 2 — would increase harmonic tension, while a change from example 2 to example 1 — both superimposed groups of thirds — would be a great release of such tension.

EXERCISE

Where and how are clusters used in 'Majority'? (The recording of this song is on Record 8, side 2 band 3 and the score is in *Scores 7*.)

DISCUSSION

The beginning (p. 8 systems 1–5) and the end (p. 10 systems 2–3). Both white-note and black-note clusters are used; all are large and heavy, producing a massive effect. Sometimes the clusters are employed purely for harmonic colour (for example, the first bar); sometimes they have melodic significance — for instance, the left hand in systems 2–3 is a 'thickening' of the repeated motive,

while at the end of the song this motive is inverted and extended.

3.2 Quarter-tone writing

Usually Ives avoided writing articles concerning specific technical matters, preferring to write experimental musical works to test a theoretical idea. However, as we have already seen, he did publish an article in 1925 (entitled 'Some "Quarter-tone" Impressions') which gives us some very clear insights into a number of his techniques of composition.

Ives argued that the quarter tone was an accepted part of early music and was only dropped when people became 'soft' in the ears. It should therefore be reintroduced, but

> The assimilation of quarter tones with what we have now into some reasonable and satisfactory basic plan will be, it seems to me, along harmonic lines, with the

melodic coming as a kind of collateral, simultaneous perhaps, and just as important, but very closely bound up with the former—in a sense, opposite to the way our present system has developed.[1]

The mutual dependence of melody and harmony in any new system of writing was a central theme in Ives' musical thinking; it may remind you of Schoenberg and twelve-note music in general, though the results in Ives are very different. He returned to the subject later in the same article:

> It seems to me that a pure quarter-tone melody needs a pure quarter-tone harmony not only to back it up but to help generate it.[2]

Thus it would be unthinkable to have quarter-tone melodic embellishments if the harmonies that supported that melody were not given a similar treatment, and it was this point that prevented Ives from using quarter tones to any great extent in any of his major works. If the instruments available were not capable of playing the music, that type of music would have to go unwritten.

Ives experimented with a specially constructed quarter-tone piano—an instrument with two keyboards, the upper of which was tuned a quarter-tone higher than the other—as well as trying out chords on two separate pianos tuned a quarter-tone apart. He was able to convince himself that some chord progressions were quite satisfactory for the formation of an hierarchical system of tonality and as such were ideally suited to a new harmonic and melodic language. He wrote *Three Quarter-Tone Pieces* in 1924–25 for a quarter-tone piano and examples of his use of this particular harmonic language can also be found in the second movement of the Fourth Symphony. Here the quarter-tone music is restricted to the strings since they have the least number of technical and mechanical difficulties in producing it.

EXERCISE

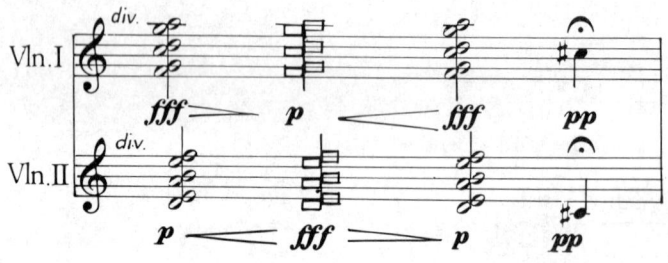

square notes = quarter-tone sharp

What is happening harmonically in this passage?

DISCUSSION

First and second violins between them play a complete white-note cluster spanning a twelfth. They then move up a quarter tone, then down to the original chord.

Naturally Ives realized the limitations of quarter-tone music, and the need for specially constructed instruments and new techniques of playing were high on the list of such restrictions. However, the main drawback, he felt, would be the ears and

---

1 Charles Ives, *Essays Before a Sonata and Other Writings.* H. Boatwright, (ed.), Calder & Boyars 1969, p. 109. (Hereafter referred to as 'Boatwright'.)

2 Boatwright, p. 110.

minds of performers, critics, and audiences who looked on music as something to help them relax rather than something to which they must really listen.

> . . . in other words, consonance has had a monopolistic tyranny, for this one principal reason: it is easy for the ear and mind to use and know them . . . The old fight of evolution—the one-syllable soft-eared boys are still on too many boards, chairs, newspapers, and concert stages![1]

3.3   Polytonality and polyrhythm

Grove's Dictionary describes polytonality as 'the simultaneous superimposition of more than two keys . . . Chords or a melodic line or lines definitely related to one key centre are heard against chords or a counterpoint belonging to another, each key group being free to go its own way.'[2] Such independence of movement had obviously been developed by Ives in his early training (by exercises such as playing a melody in one key and its accompaniment in another—a simple bitonal structure), but it was a technique that he deliberately cultivated.

At first it appears that his serious use of polytonality was derived from rhythmic thinking.

> Rhythm is a thing perhaps more to be felt than tones are. To feel several rhythms together and hear them as such is not as difficult as it is for one man to play them. As a rule, probably more than three rhythms on the piano is ineffective—and perhaps three or four, in pieces for two players, as in a violin and piano sonata, or music for voice and piano.[3]

However, despite the comment that such rhythmic memorizing was not particularly difficult in a limited number of parts, Ives suggested that it was a considerable feat to use more than three independent patterns:

> I have with much practice been able to keep five, and even six, rhythms going in my mind at once so that I can hear each one naturally by leaning toward it, changing the ear in each measure—and I think this is the more natural way of hearing and learning the use of and feeling for rhythms, than by writing them and playing from them on paper, which shows the exact position of each note in relation to each other, in the eye.[4]

The solution, Ives felt, lay in massed strength rather than in individual effort.

> To have polyrhythm rise to its full strength there must be one or a group of players to each rhythm—(by rhythm here I mean something which is only a part of rhythm in its bigger sense—various times of beat to one unit). And each group, if possible, should be of different tonal sounds—for example: strings, brass, drums, bells, wood, and the various kinds of percussion instruments, each to each meter.[5]

It is, of course, only a small step from playing these independent group rhythmic patterns to asking the performers to play in separate keys also. Thus for Ives polytonal writing was not just a matter of combining 'chords or a melodic line or lines definitely

---

1   *Memos*, p. 110.
2   *Grove's Dictionary of Music and Musicians*, fifth edition, Eric Blom (ed.), Macmillan 1954, vol. VIII, p. 502.
3   *Memos*, p. 123.
4   *Memos*, p. 125.
5   *Memos*, p. 124.

related to one key centre' with 'chords or a counterpoint belonging to another'; it was the simultaneous superimposition of several complete musical entities — almost a type of collage. Rudolph Reti has suggested that

> The polyphony of Schoenberg and his followers, for instance, much as it may surpass previous ways of formation with regard to harmonic concepts and patterns of grouping, still remains a polyphony of single lines, even if diversified, melodically autonomous lines. So also in Strawinsky's polyphonic web . . . But Ives for the first time in history establishes, or at least tries to establish, in quite a number of compositions a *polyphony of groups*. A polyphony in which the elements are not lines but full musical entities which carry within themselves their harmonic and contrapuntal life.[1]

At some times this is carried so far as to lead the composer John Cage to write of 'the mud of Ives': a complex seemingly chaotic total effect within which the individual details are unimportant. This happens most often in orchestral works, for obvious reasons, the songs and piano music tending to be somewhat clearer, but there are nevertheless good examples of polytonal and polyrhythmic effects in pieces like 'Majority' and 'An Election' (see *Scores 7*). The close and, especially, the opening of 'Majority' show the use of two independent polyphonic groups (basically the two staves of the piano part). Rhythmically they are quite distinct. Notice also that when one is made up mostly of black notes, the other tends to stress white notes (p. 8 system 4 for example). The behaviour of the bass, systems 5–6 is interesting too. Against a steady minim–crotchet flow, it gradually, and autonomously, speeds up from semibreves to triplet minims, crotchets, quintuplet crotchets and septuplet minims. The beginning and ending of 'An Election' are similar in many ways (see p. 5 systems 1–2 and 3–5, p. 7 systems 4–5). Here polyrhythmic effects are supplemented with clear bitonal chord constructions (p. 5 systems 4–5, p. 7 system 17). Another striking polytonal chord construction occurs in the second last bar from the end of 'Majority': Ives piles up a huge aggregation of B flat, B natural, C and D flat, triads.

EXERCISE

Look at the passage in 'An Election' from p. 6 system 5 to p. 7 system 1 second bar, and listen to it (Record 8 side 2 band 2). Describe the polyrhythmic and polytonal techniques used here.

DISCUSSION

In the first bar the voice divides into crotchet units, while until the last chord the piano is in 3/8. From the second half of p. 6 system 6 on, the music is polytonal *and* polyrhythmic. The voice is based on G, the piano l.h. on F (until the last bar) and the r.h., though chromatic, stresses B. Voice and l.h. both suggest 4/4, but the r.h. has a repeated group of *nine* semiquavers which inevitably overlaps the other strands irregularly.

3.4 New chords and new structural relationships

We have already seen how Ives produced various new chord formations by the introduction of smaller sub-divisions of the octave (the quarter tone), by the logical extension of the conventional system of thirds to create clusters and by the superimposition of a number of keys (polytonality) to produce composite chord structures.

---

1   Rudolph Reti, *Tonality in Modern Music*, Collier Books, New York 1962, p. 173.

There were, however, a number of other techniques that he commonly used, although no one formation could be singled out as the 'typical Ives chord'.

In his song 'Soliloquy' (appropriately subtitled 'A Study in 7ths and Other Things') we can see a number of these alternative ways of constructing harmonic configurations all in the space of a single page. This song appears in *Scores 7* though it is not included on the records.

After a long, recitative-like bar accompanied by chords built up by the multiple super-imposition of thirds, Ives begins a section in which the chords in the piano part are compilations of sevenths (bars 3 and 5) or (its inversion) ninths (bars 2 and 4). Bars 6 and 7 then present a forceful display: a progression of chords built successively on minor sevenths, fifths, fourths, thirds, whole tones and, lastly, semitones. This series is then repeated in the reverse (expanding) order.

sevenths fifths fourths thirds whole- semitones
tones

Despite their differing intervallic content, each of these chords has been constructed in the traditional way: subsequent notes have been added above a predetermined bass note and the chord is quite literally 'built up'. Now, however, we are shown chords which have been made from the top note downwards. Once again they are constructed out of sevenths (bars 8 and 10) or ninths (bars 9 and 11). The song concludes with a single chord that sums up the entire harmonic construction in one statement. It is a compilation of fourths, thirds, whole tones and semitones (which of course imply major sevenths and minor ninths).

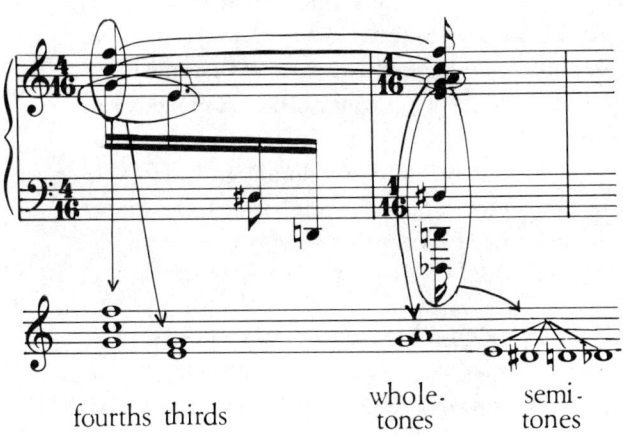

fourths thirds   whole-   semitones   tones

EXERCISE

What can you say about (a) the melodic shape of the vocal line in bars 2–11; (b) the structure of bars 2–11?

DISCUSSION

(a) The interval of a seventh is prominent throughout, making the shape very angular (note the song's subtitle, 'A Study in 7ths and Other Things'). The pitches are very varied; indeed bars 2–4 present a twelve-note set — all twelve chromatic semitones are used with no repetition. The pitch selection in bars 5–7 and 8–10 is almost as rigorous.

(b)   The chords in bars 8–11 are pretty well the same as those in bars 2–5, only back to front (retrograded). We have already seen that bar 7 is a retrograde of bar 6. So, harmonically, the whole of bars 2–11 is constructed as a palindrome. As in the vocal line the interval of a seventh (or its inversion the ninth) is the most prominent interval. In addition there is a logical rhythmic scheme which also forms a palindrome. The time signatures (following the vocal part) read 5/16 6/16 7/16 8/16 5/16 || 5/16 8/16 7/16 6/16 5/16.

Taking into account the prominence of the seventh in the slow introduction too (the two pivotal chords are built on D flat and D natural respectively), you can see that 'Soliloquy' is very tightly constructed. Ives was not as 'chaotic' a composer as is sometimes thought; in fact such seemingly 'mathematical' methods are quite common in his music, though not usually audible. 'Soliloquy' was written in 1907, that is, before Schoenberg and Webern were using twelve-note chromaticism, melodic angularity and inversion and retrograde techniques in comparable ways.

Ives was also interested in new kinds of tonality formed through relating chords, new and familiar, in original ways. He began experimenting with altered chord relationships

> . . . sometime before May 1902 (when I resigned as a nice organist and gave up music). When a man has played at church services for ten or fifteen years steadily he gets slightly used to the three fundamental triads, in the hymns and anthems as well as in the plain chants.[1]

In an attempt to overcome the boredom of continually playing these triads Ives tells us how, in the third movement of the Set for Theatre or Chamber Orchestra

> . . . I tried to find three chords that might be used in a similar or parallel sense to the usual tonic, dominant and subdominant — a combination of chords that would not be undignified, that would have some musical sense and relation, and about which melodies or counterpoints could be used as a natural outcome from these combinations. In this movement, D flat was taken as the main chord (or tonic), and B flat (in this case a tone above the dominant A flat) was used as the dominant, and the chord of E major (a tone below the subdominant G flat) was used as the subdominant. These chords have a note in common with the tonic, and B flat used as the dominant seems to have a stronger resolving value than the subdominant, E major.[2]

Although he later described this movement as 'not only *not* complicated but so simple and reasonable that it might be called a close relation to stupidity (or arestology)'[3], it gives us a clear idea of the scientific pattern of his researches into the subject of new chordal relationships. A similar thoroughness is displayed in his experiments concerning the progression of quarter-tone chords. In this excerpt from 'Some "Quarter-Tone" Impressions' the word '(quarter)' indicates that the note is to be played on the upper keyboard of a specially constructed piano and will therefore sound a quarter of a tone sharp.

> Again, the chord C G E (quarter) B (quarter) seems to me stronger in itself than the one we have outlined above, but the narrow interval B (quarter) with the octave makes it rather impracticable, especially in inversions.

1   *Memos*, p. 57.
2   *Memos*, p. 57.
3   *Memos*, p. 58.

Another chord which might do as a fundamental is C E G (quarter) A sharp (quarter), but it appears to me that the assertiveness of the major third at the bottom throws the mind into a kind of diatonic expectancy which the upper intervals resist . . .

There is little more choice if a secondary chord corollary to the fundamental is to be found. The chord in itself, I think, should give a feeling of less finality than the first. It should be absorbed readily by the fundamental, it should have lesser intervals, and, in general, a contrasting character, and a note in common with the primary chord . . .[1]

EXERCISE

Listen to 'Majority' from p. 8 last system to p. 10 first system and study it in the score. Describe the methods of chord construction Ives uses.

DISCUSSION

1 Up to 6/8 'Moderately' section: almost entirely constructed from fourths.
2 Then up to 'a little slower': minim clusters

otherwise mostly built from sevenths and ninths.
3 From 'The Masses are yearning' to 'Hope of the World': plentiful sevenths and seconds but also prominent tritones and augmented fifths.
4 From 'Slowly': large aggregations of thirds, usually topped with whole tones

etc

3.5   The use of harmonics

One further set of experiments that became a part of Ives' musical language and formed the technical basis for a number of works was his research into the uses of harmonics or overtones. Any note produced by any musical instrument is a composite sound consisting of many simultaneously produced pure tones called harmonics, over-tones or partials. The lowest sounding of these is called the fundamental and, since it is the loudest, it determines the actual pitch heard. The frequencies of the other harmonics are mathematically exact multiples of the frequency of the fundamental, and the intervals between these harmonics get smaller as the series ascends to infinity. However, not all these notes are in tune according to any scale actually in use, and the untrained ear does not usually detect any of these harmonics.

Ives' use of this (often unheard but always present) sound material began in his days as a church organist. Because it is the most complex musical instrument under the control of one performer and has a wide range of pitches, contrasting tonal colours and dynamic ranges, the organ proved to be a most useful 'workshop' instrument for Ives, as we have already seen from the number of works that commenced as organ voluntaries. His early experiments involved the use of the softer organ stops to

1 Boatwright, p. 113.

reinforce the harmonics of some of the stronger ranks and by so doing to provide an accompaniment to the melody line that these were playing. The following example shows the end of a hymn interlude based on the melody *Nearer My God to Thee*, which is played in the bass while the accompanying chords form part of the harmonic series attendant on each note.

A technique such as this provides an answer to the problems of finding a logical and yet workable relationship between the melody and its accompaniment and at the same time it provides an automatic means of arriving at a satisfactory chord progression for any given melodic statement. It is, however, mainly a feature of Ives' earlier music and is not at all common in his instrumental writing.

3.6 Summary

It can be seen that Ives was struggling to find some of the musical possibilities he spoke of earlier: the 'wider scales' and 'new combinations of tone' in the melodic field and 'new keys, and more keys, and beats, and phrases together' in the harmonic and rhythmic domains. This struggle was not the result of an emotional 'crisis' or a sudden inspiration, but of carefully planned and well conducted research and experiment. It led him to believe that further developments were possible and he attempted to discover some of these possibilities and to make use of them in his own compositions.

> The more one studies and listens and tries to find out all he can in various ways, technically, mathematically, acoustically and aurally, [the more] he begins to feel (and more than that, actually know and sense) that the world of tonal vibrations, in its relation to the physiological structure of the human ear, has unthought of (because untried) possibilities for man to know and grow by—greater and more transcendent than what has too easily and thoughtlessly [been] called a natural law! Just a few months' study of what can be found in the tables of acoustical vibrations—pure, tempered, differences of overtones, beats, etc.—as found in Helmholtz et al—and it will be realized that nature's laws are greater than a mere plagal cadence. [1]

EXERCISE

Study 'An Election', from 'Then the timid . . .' to 'Out of his hole' (*Scores* 7, pp. 6 and 7). Which of the technical features discussed above are contained in these bars?

DISCUSSION

The most obvious is the use of clusters in the lower stave of the fourth, fifth, eighth and ninth bars of the extract. They are all white-note clusters. The smaller (two-note) clusters in the right hand in bar 5 and in the bass of bars 6 and 7 are used to 'thicken' the melodic line in the first case and to add weight to the bass note in the second.

1 *Memos*, p. 197.

We have already commented on the polytonal and polyrhythmic construction of 'Then the timid smiled': if you didn't remember this, look back at the discussion on p. 24 above. The use of bitonality in bar 4 of the extract is also fairly easy to see—the accidentals in the right hand and voice contrast with the white-note clusters in the left hand. The upper part suggests the scale of F sharp minor by stating six of its seven notes:

while the lower part outlines the scale of C major with five notes:

C D E F G A B
* * * * *

Tonal 'layering' continues in bar 5, though the tonalities of the two parts are less clear, and bars 6–7: here l.h. is in an F/C orbit while r.h. revolves around F sharp/B. Polyrhythmic construction is used in bars 8–9:

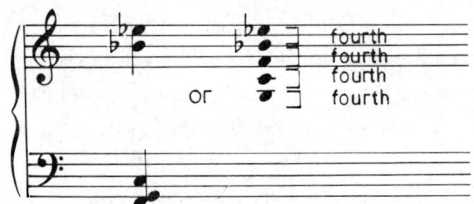

The chord construction in bars 6–7 is also worth noting. Instead of thirds Ives has used chords built of fourths, the notes of those chords then being rearranged to suit the shape of the hand. The first chord of the bar is an easy example to follow:

One last point which has to do with an aspect of Ives not so far mentioned: in the third bar of this excerpt, when 'the timid smiled and looked relieved', Ives has inserted a very obvious, textbook tonal cadence in G major—for the relief of the timid listeners who like their music '. . . so smooth [that] our ears must become like unto feather beds, our muscles all drop out, and we have to have false-teeth ears to hear it with!'[1] He does much the same earlier in the song at 'natural enough' and 'that's the easy way!' As we shall see later, this 'programmatic' use of material, this fondness for 'quoting', in the widest sense of the word, is characteristic of Ives. It is part of his eclecticism—which in turn stems from his belief that 'the fabric of existence weaves itself whole . . . There can be nothing "*exclusive*" about a substantial art.'[2]

1   *Memos*, p. 101.

2   Quoted in H. Wiley Hitchcock, *Ives*, Oxford University Press 1977, p. 6.

4   The *Concord* Sonata

When Ives privately published the *Second Pianoforte Sonata ('Concord, Mass., 1840–60')*, the *Essays Before a Sonata* (both 1920), and his collection of *114 Songs* (1922), he was attempting to give to the general public those works that he considered to be the most representative of his style, the most important in his collection of manuscripts and the most interesting to hear. We can therefore learn a great deal about his musical style, his technical abilities and his musical philosophy from a study of some of these works.

The *Concord* Sonata is a particularly valuable work for any such study, partly because it is one of the best documented of Ives' large-scale works and partly because the limitations placed on the composer by the instrument make this sonata a relatively easy work to comprehend. These limitations include restrictions on the size of the chords and the complexity of the rhythmic structures due to the physical characteristics and abilities of the performer (it is, for example, quite impossible to ask him to play more than ten notes simultaneously without the use of clusters played with the arm) and limitations on the complexity of musical thought when there is only one basic tonal colour — 'piano' tone — available. An orchestral work, for example, may be much more complex in its interweaving of independent melodic lines because these pitch strands are naturally separated by the differing orchestral colours, but this technique has only a very limited application in piano writing.

As well as these features, the *Concord* Sonata offers us a further bonus — the *Essays Before a Sonata*. These occupy a prominent position among Ives' literary efforts. Of course, we may often read the writings of a creative artist in the hope of finding what it is that separates such a man from his fellows and (if this is our only reason for reading them) be sadly disappointed. Most of Ives' literary works do not deal with music directly; if he was concerned with a musical point he usually wrote music. But he used words to provide his listeners with a general philosophical background and support for his compositions and when this is associated with the music we may be more able to see his unique development as a composer.

4.1   The score of the Sonata

The score you are using is a reproduction of the original edition, published privately by Ives in 1920. Later he produced a revised version, published in 1947, and it is this which is the basis of Ronald Lumsden's recording — though he introduces one or two variations. You will notice discrepancies between your score and the record, but in view of Ives' own attitudes to the performance of *Concord*, this doesn't matter:

> Some of the passages now played [by him] haven't been written out . . . and I don't know as I shall ever write them out, as it may take away the daily pleasure of playing this music and seeing it grow and feeling that it is not finished. (I may always have the pleasure of not finishing it.)[1]

Indeed the discrepancies may have the virtue of enlightening you to the nature of Ives' approach to notation and performance.

In your score you will notice there are printed extracts from the *Essays Before a Sonata*. These are very useful — indeed almost essential — for an understanding of the music, and I shall refer to them often.

---

1   *Memos*, pp. 79–80.

4.2   The format of the Sonata

Ives described this work as a 'group of four pieces, called a sonata for want of a more exact name, as the form, perhaps substance, does not justify it.'[1] The four 'pieces' (or movements) are entitled 'Emerson', 'Hawthorne', 'The Alcotts' and 'Thoreau', and the whole is 'an attempt to present (one person's) impression of the spirit of transcendentalism that is associated in the minds of many with Concord, Mass, of over a half-century ago.'[2] We are therefore dealing with music that is a series of impressionistic sketches instead of a classically formed sonata. The impressionism, however, is not that of Debussy or Ravel, which portrays events, situations, sensory perceptions. Instead we are dealing with an impressionism that seeks to present a philosophy and an ideal — an attempt to use music to express what may be impossible to put into words.

New England Transcendentalism is difficult to define. It is associated with men like Emerson, Thoreau, Bronson Alcott and Hawthorne, but it never solidified into a consistent body of doctrine. Broadly speaking, the Transcendentalists were united in drawing inspiration from German Idealism (particularly Kant) and from Romantics such as Coleridge and Wordsworth, and they all stressed the importance of intuition (as against reason or empirical observation) as a means of cognition. They shared

> a vague yet exalting conception of the godlike nature of the human spirit and an insistence on the authority of individual conscience; a related respect for the significance and autonomy of every facet of human experience within the organic totality of life . . . [a vision of] nature conceived not as a vast machine demanding impersonal manipulation but as an organism, a symbol and analogue of mind . . .[3]

Of course the use of 'programme' music was not new: the writers of nineteenth-century tone poems thrived on it. What was new was the use of programme music for such an abstract purpose, and it is this that leads us to see that Ives had a different idea of what such music is, and what it may (or may not) be able to do.

> Can a tune literally present a stone wall with vines on it or even with nothing on it, though it (the tune) be made by a genius whose power of objective contemplation is in the highest state of development? Can it be done by anything short of an act of mesmerism on the part of the composer or an act of kindness on the part of the listener?[4]

Whatever type of programme music a composer writes, he faces a problem, according to Ives:

> Does the success of program music depend more upon the program than upon the music? If it does, what is the use of the music? If it does not, what is the use of the program?[5]

Finally, after a long series of questions and answers (and almost as many new questions as he supplies answers) Ives reduces the problem to what he sees as the real essence of music:

> . . . the translation of an artistic intuition into musical sounds approving and reflecting, or endeavouring to approve and reflect, a 'moral goodness', a 'high vitality' etc., or any other human attribute — mental, moral or spiritual.[6]

---

1   Boatwright, p. xxv.
2   Boatwright, p. xxv.
3   *The Encyclopedia of Philosophy*, Collier-Macmillan 1967, Vol. 5, pp. 479–80.
4   Boatwright, p. 3.
5   Boatwright, p. 4.
6   Boatwright, pp. 7–8.

This, then, is what we can expect in the *Concord* Sonata: an attempted translation of Ives' artistic intuition concerning a group of people who lived in the town of Concord, Massachusetts, between 1840 and 1860.

4.3 Third movement—'The Alcotts'

We will begin our study of the *Concord* Sonata with this movement as it is the simplest in its form and musical content. *I would suggest that you play through the movement a couple of times first (Record 9, side 2 band 1).*

The *Essays* introduce us to only three characters and give a brief sketch of the Alcott family life. The people are old Bronson Alcott, described as 'Concord's greatest talker', his neighbour (and critic) Sam Staples and Alcott's daughter Louisa May, author of *Little Women*, who 'seldom misses the chance to bring out the moral of a homely virtue'. Father and daughter obviously have certain characteristics in common, for Ives adds that 'The power of repetition was to them a natural means of illustration'.[1] The brief suggestion of the Alcott family life includes the statement (see the introduction in your score)

> And there sits the little old spinnet piano Sophia Thoreau gave to the Alcott children, on which Beth played the old Scotch airs and played at the *Fifth Symphony*.

The concluding words of the essay on the Alcotts are also of interest to us.

> And so we won't try to reconcile the music sketch of the Alcotts with much besides the memory of that home under the elms—the Scotch songs and the family hymns that were sung at the end of each day . . . though there may be an attempt to catch something of that common sentiment . . . a conviction in the power of the common soul . . .

Earlier Ives stresses the 'homeliness' theme, talking of 'that common virtue lying at the height and root of all the Concord divinities . . . a spiritual sturdiness . . . a kind of common triad of the New England homestead . . .' The only other information that Ives offers is to be found in his *Memos*:

> . . . the Alcott piece tries to catch something of old man Alcott's—the great talker's—sonorous thought[2]

and the musical expression of that 'sonorous thought' is one of the central reference points of the movement, expressed as the key of A flat and played by the left hand.

> The left hand is in A flat—in that key—no other key—keeps that key—is that key—it intends, does [is] meant to do that, couldn't do anything else, and will always put the player's left-hand-mind in that nice key of A flat and nothing else (for old man Alcott likes to talk in A flat, and Sam Staples likes to have his say over the fence in B flat) . . .[3]

The reference to Beethoven's Fifth Symphony in the *Essays* gives us our first real musical clue to the construction of this movement. An examination of Beethoven's opening theme reveals a close relationship between it and Ives' beginning to 'The Alcotts'.

1 Boatwright, pp. 45–46.
2 *Memos*, p. 199.
3 *Memos*, p. 191.

Ives quickly converts his theme into a statement of Beethoven's motive by means of several small rhythmic changes — a transformation that occurs very early in the movement. The original opening is given a sharper articulation (and a closer resemblance to Beethoven's motive) by the use of a rest at the start of the figure and a tie at the end to prevent the reiteration of the last note (p. 53 system 3).

Further adjustments and developments follow until the original Beethoven theme is sounded prominently in all voices (p. 54).

A study of the accompaniment to this opening theme produces several more surprises. The bass, for example, presents us with the first line of the hymn tune *Laudate Dominum* ('O Praise Ye the Lord') with one small addition for harmonic reasons:

Obviously this is a reference to the 'family hymns that were sung at the end of each day', while the 'old Scotch airs' played by Beth may be represented by a fragment of the Christmas carol *Figgy Pudding* ('We Wish You a Merry Christmas') which occurs at the same time.

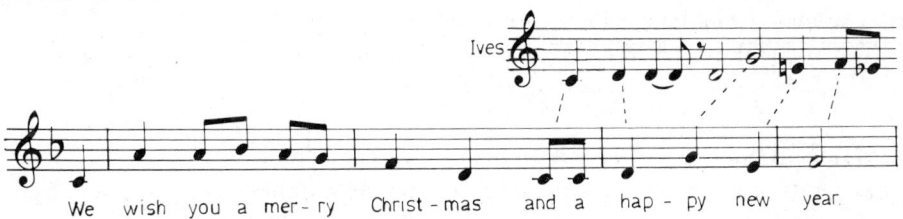

Thus we have a nearly simultaneous statement of three of the musical elements discussed in the essay within the first few bars of the movement.

EXERCISE

Can you locate Bronson Alcott's sonorous (but repetitious) speech (which, remember, is in A flat), and Sam Staples 'having his say' (in B flat)?

DISCUSSION

Bronson Alcott follows immediately after the opening thematic statement. The chord of A flat, given one particular rhythmic articulation, is repeated nine consecutive times in the bass, with three further statements of the chord without the rhythm, as if the old man had come at last to a definite conclusion.

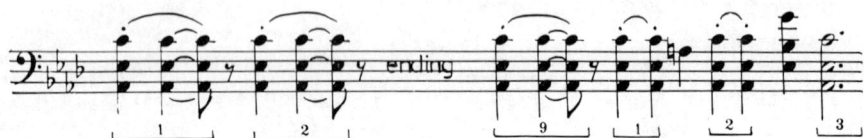

Over the top of this, Sam Staples has 'his say over the fence in B flat':

We can now see a beautiful example of one of Ives' favourite techniques — polytonal counterpoint — effortlessly used to illustrate the different characteristics of the many elements that made up the life-style of the Alcotts. We can also begin to see his 'collage' technique of constructing a work from segments of various melodies (his own as well as those of other composers), each of which retains its individuality while being subordinated to the musical whole.

I would suggest that you now listen to the whole movement once again, trying to follow these features, and also sort out the form of the piece.

EXERCISE

How would you describe the form of the movement? Is the structure clear or not?

DISCUSSION

At first hearing it may seem rather rambling and 'formless'. It doesn't fall at all clearly into one of the traditional forms and there is no straight repetition. Ives disliked obvious repeats, preferring continuously evolving structures, which are always revealing variations and relationships in the material. In 'The Alcotts' the E flat section (p. 55 system 3 onwards), a beautiful 'idealization' of nineteenth-century 'parlour' piano music, sounds very much like a 'middle section', though it grows without check into more complex material (p. 56 system 4) and is followed by only a brief reminiscence of the opening themes (p. 57 system 1 last few notes, more clearly, systems 5 and 6). However, the rest of the movement is entirely based on these two opening themes ('Beethoven' and 'Sam Staples'); moreover the two are linked—compare these rhythmic patterns:

While not banging a drum about it, then, the bulk of the movement is based on one 'transcending' idea.

Ives' comments:

> The continuity of this music is more a process of natural tonal diversification and distribution than of natural tonal repetition and resolution. Often the roots or the beginning and end of a passage or cycle are not literally the beginnings or ends—but combinations of tone that can and do stand for them, if not to the eye, to the ear and mind after sufficient familiarity.[1]

> And when the Nice Old Ladies say 'no design—formless—all music should have design and form'—Yes, Sarah, but not your designs and forms—No Siree! In this Sonata they're spitting about—there is design—somewhat more than there should be, it seemed to me—and the form is obvious, but it isn't drabbed on every milestone on the way *up* or *to* or *on*—it takes care of itself, so to speak, and isn't yanked back every thirty-two measures by those nice apron strings hanging on the classroom scroll.[2]

4.4   First movement—'Emerson'

As we may expect, the *Essays* again give us some veiled clues to help in the unravelling of this complicated movement. The information is not as precise as it was in 'The Alcotts' because we are dealing with a far more complex character, the writer and philosopher Ralph Waldo Emerson (1803–82). However, there are quite a few signposts.

EXERCISE

Read the three-page introduction to the Emerson movement printed in the score and taken from the Essays. *Listen to the movement on your record (Side 1 band 1).* Then list those qualities attributed to Emerson by Ives which appear to be reflected in the music.

DISCUSSION

'. . . an invader of the unknown,—America's greatest explorer of the spiritual immensities . . .' (What I feel about the music.)
'. . . describing the inevitable *struggle* in the soul's uprise . . .' (My italics.)

1   *Memos*, p. 195.
2   *Memos*, p. 196.

'. . . standing on a summit, at the door of the infinite . . .' (Again this to me describes Ives in this movement.)

'Emerson wrings the neck of any law . . .' (Compare the music's lack of obvious design.)

'. . . Emerson must be dubbed an optimist . . .' (The music is always strong and positive.)

'Emerson is more interested in what he perceives than in his expression of it.' (That is, 'substance' not 'manner', a favourite theme of Ives.)

'To think hard and deeply and to say what is thought, regardless of consequences, may produce a first impression, either of great translucence, or of great muddiness . . .' (The music exactly.)

'Emerson wrote by sentences or phrases, rather than by logical sequence . . . the large unity of a series of particular aspects of a subject, rather than . . . the continuity of its expression.' (This seems to me how the music is organized.)

'. . . one of Beethoven's greatest messages . . . the soul of humanity knocking at the door of the Divine mysteries . . .' (I hope you spotted the 'Beethoven' theme, previously used in 'The Alcotts' movement.)

The kind of phrases Ives uses in his essay may lead us to expect some new musical discoveries, some unusual processes being applied in the invasion of the 'unknown', and we are not disappointed. Ives, on Emerson's behalf, certainly paints 'his discoveries in masses' (in this case, masses of notes), and 'with any colour that may lie at hand', even though such expression may be physically taxing to the performer and an equal mental strain on the listener.

Historically, the 'Emerson' movement began its life as a series of sketches for an overture with piano, but this work was never scored, or even finished. Describing the translation of this overture into the first movement of the *Concord* Sonata, Ives wrote:

> The Overture . . . seems more like a Piano Concerto with sort of cadenzas. Quite a little of the Overture [is] not in the Sonata. Because [it's] not in the Sonata may not mean that it ought to be—or that it was left out by mistake . . . The Overture (what is left) and the Sonata (in the book) are, in some ways, more like two separate and different pieces on some of the same texts, than the same piece in different forms. [1]

One other comment by Ives may make the listener's task easier:

> Though the Emerson movement started as a kind of piano concerto, the orchestra was the world and people hearing, and the piano cadenza was Emerson . . . [2]

Although this comment was obviously made when the composer was thinking back to the unfinished Overture, it still tells us a lot about the first movement of the *Concord* Sonata: it explains, for example, the sectionalized construction and the sudden juxtapositions of virtuosic flourishes and leaps with more solid, chordal writing.

As stated earlier, the essay on Emerson leads us to expect musical innovations. Right from the start of the movement we find a type of musical expression that is frequently without barlines. This of course means that it is freed from the almost obligatory accent on the first note of every bar and from the near-tyrannical metric pulse so

1 *Memos*, p. 203.
2 *Memos*, p. 189.

common in music of the seventeenth, eighteenth and nineteenth centuries. Henry and Sidney Cowell speak of

> . . . cases where there is no particular metrical organization, regular or irregular. Here Ives leaves out the metrical signature, and he has either no bar lines at all or else he sets them irregularly where he wishes the impression of a first beat. This is a prose concept of rhythm; it is also related to the idea that different stresses may be given by different performers, all of them right. The *Emerson* movement of the *Concord Sonata* affords an example.

> In some cases one may feel a constant uninterrupted succession of strong beats . . . But usually one feels that Ives hopes to induce the performer not to be too bound by one way of organizing strong and weak beats, playing the passages now one way, now another.[1]

EXERCISE

Let's look at an example, what I would call the first paragraph, which ends with the rest almost at the end of p. 5. Compare Ives' use of barlines on pp. 1–2 and p. 4. For what purposes is he using them in the two cases?

DISCUSSION

On pp. 1–2 they simply seem to mark the beginnings of sentences. Thus the bulk of p. 1 consists of three related sentences, each of which starts with an upward rush, followed by a long descent. (The rush is longer in the first sentence than the subsequent two, and the final descent is longer and more complex than the preceding ones. But the pattern is clear.) The placing of the barlines helps the performer to articulate this structure. On the other hand, most of p. 4 is metrical music (in 4/4) and the barlines here are mostly used conventionally.

Note that at some other times when the music is fairly metrical (for example, p. 5 first two systems) Ives does *not* use barlines. This is presumably because, despite the clear 3/4 structure of this passage, it could be phrased and accented in several different ways, and Ives wants to encourage this.

EXERCISE

Throughout the barline-free sections the accenting is very irregular. Can you identify two other techniques used in the first paragraph to help de-regularize the rhythmic continuity?

DISCUSSION

1 Cross-accenting between contrapuntal lines (e.g. bottom system p. 3: r.h. in 4/4, l.h. syncopated), which sometimes turns into quite complex polyrhythms (second system p. 2 is a good example; or third system p. 3 — here is how I would 'bar' that passage, starting at the second minim:

1 Cowell, *op. cit.*, p. 172.

I am sure others would do it differently—but at any rate it cannot be played other than polyrhythmically).

2 Changes of tempo, which are very frequent.

The concept of playing a work differently every time was important to Ives. In his *Memos about the Concord Sonata (1913–1929)* he writes

> And some ask, 'what do you mean not to play literally?' Several reasons . . . One [reason is] that [it's] better not to—or [you] don't have to (which is the best [reason]) play everything and piece and measure the same way every time—not as Josey Hoffman et al play Beethoven, this nice little note just this way, etc.—Ta ta—making Beethoven a lady-bird etc.
>
> Play it before breakfast   like ____!
> ,, ,, after   ,,   ,, ____!
> ,, ,,   ,,   digging potatoes ,, ____!
>
> In fact, these notes, marks, and near pictures of sounds etc. are in a kind of way a platform for the player to make his own speeches on. And as I tried to infer in the book, in various places, that Emerson, Thoreau especially, and the others perhaps less so, weren't static, rule-making, do-as-I'm-told professors,—to me their thoughts, substance and inspiration change and grow . . .[1]

Again, in a letter of 11 October 1935 to the pianist John Kirkpatrick he wrote

> However, do whatever seems natural or best to *you*, though not necessarily the same way each time. The music, in its playing as well as in its substance, should have some of Emerson's freedom in action and thought—of the explorer 'taking the ultimate of today as the first of tomorrow's new series'. It is said that Emerson seldom gave any of his lectures in exactly the same way, and that the published essays were not kept to literally.[2]

Naturally, playing a work differently every time will have the benefit of highlighting varying features in every performance. In the case of the 'Emerson' movement the idea of variation by the performer may well be vital to our understanding of the work for:

> The notes hold into the next general thought, as thoughts do—every thought hasn't a clothes-pin between it and the next—they go on and up. Emerson's thought was usually a part of the before and afterward—not little miniature ideas in frames, to be read easily and put down, etc. It was bigger and greater and higher than a one-line picture on paper. These longer notes on the lesser beats, of course, are helped by the pedal, but this is a poor substitute for what I had in mind—(that is, what Emerson, Thoreau, etc. had in mind, and what I tried to get out of my system in 'tones' or in 'sounds' if you like—call it music or not, it makes no difference)—and then the pedal . . . when lifted, stops the thought-sounds, which ought to be thought of continuing to their natural ends.[3]

We are thus dealing with music that has a number of possible interpretations and that offers various different levels of 'meaning' to both performers and listener. How should you listen to it? As Wiley Hitchcock writes, it is 'difficult to follow conceptually (though not viscerally)'[4], and I suggest you listen many times to 'Emerson', letting it wash over you and allowing it to reveal the web of thematic connections. To help, here is an (abbreviated!) thematic guide, showing the most important themes.

1 *Memos*, pp. 191–92.
2 *Memos*, pp. 200–1.
3 *Memos*, pp. 188–89.
4 Hitchcock, *Ives*, p. 51.

38

You will recognize [C] and [D] from 'The Alcotts' (they are 'Sam Staples' and 'Beethoven' respectively); and the variants of [D] which I quote appear there too (see, for example, p. 53 system 3).

4.5 Second movement—'Hawthorne'

Named after the novelist and short-story writer Nathaniel Hawthorne (1804–1864) this movement began its musical life with a series of false starts and rewrites. The information that Ives gives us in his *Memos* is rather like a large jigsaw puzzle in which many of the vital pieces are missing and even after careful study we may still find it difficult to comprehend the total picture.

> The second movement, *Hawthorne* . . . started principally with the *Celestial Railroad* idea—(in two pieces for the piano, take-offs: *The Celestial Railroad* . . . *The Slaves' Shuffle* . . . *Demons' Dance around the Pipe*—and were written on our first vacation at Pell's, September 1909)—and it was thought of at first as a piece for two pianos, or two pianos and four players. But in having the music published, it was reduced for one piano . . .[1]

The features noted by Ives can be easily seen in the score.'The Celestial Railroad' rattles along on p. 22

etc.

---

1 *Memos*, p. 81.

and the 'Slaves' Shuffle' is probably the second ragtime section which begins on p. 36

The *Demons' Dance around the Pipe* can be identified from a copy marked by Ives. On p. 23, at the end of the second line, the right hand part is marked 'demons' and the left hand 'pipe rim'. From these fragments of information it would appear that the movement started out as a set of short pictorial sections, and the *Essays* support this theory. *Read the extract from the* Essays *printed in the score before the 'Hawthorne' movement*. Ives makes it clear that he is not providing a 'comprehensive conception of Hawthorne', but rather 'an "extended fragment" trying to suggest some of his wilder, fantastical adventures into the half-childlike, half-fairylike phantasmal realms'.

Before listening to this movement and then going on to examine some of the more technical features it may be useful to read a description of the idea (or programme) behind the music, written by Ives in 1913.

> The *Magical Frost Waves* on the Berkshire dawn window—to me the *Hawthorne* movement starts with that, first on the morning window pane, then on the meadow . . . and then a boy lands on the stoop faster . . . and then he gets riding on the railroad—perhaps (but not every day) on the Celestial Railroad—then jumps over the castle wall with Feathertop . . . Then all of a sudden he is in the old churchyard—he hears the solemn old hymn, the distant bells—his old ghost friend greets him—he feels suddenly reverent in an honest boylike way . . . And then he gets hit and jumps on the railroad again and is off—he forgets the dead and dances on the Demon's pipe bowl—why can't that all be a natural part of serious music?[1]

EXERCISE

Listen to the recording of this movement (side 1 band 2) and follow the score. Note the passages that you think correspond to the images suggested by Ives in the above quotation and in the introduction in the score.

DISCUSSION

There will obviously be a number of passages that will be difficult to relate to an extra-musical programme without having a detailed knowledge of the writings of Hawthorne. Nevertheless, there are still plenty of clearly evident relationships to allow us to gain some insight into the construction of this movement.

My list would read:
pp. 21*ff*   'Frost wave'
p. 22 system 3*ff*   'Celestial Railroad'
p. 22 system 5*ff*   'Feathertop'
p. 24 systems 1–2   Boy jumps over the castle wall
p. 24 system 4*ff*   In the old churchyard
pp. 32, 33   The old hymn
pp. 34–35   The circus parade
pp. 36*ff*   'Slaves' Shuffle'

1 *Memos*, pp. 187–88.

The most easily recognizable link between the music and the programme is the 'frost-wave' opening. The groups follow a 'frost' pattern, all rather similar in basic shape but quite individual when we come to study small details. For example, the notes of the second 'wave' are repeated for the fourth, but with the D flat shortened and the last note lengthened. This type of slightly developed repetition is typical of much of Ives' musical thinking: ideas are frequently subjected to immense rhythmic changes but often these transformations take place so gradually that we may not notice them, or they are so skilfully disguised that they slip past.

It is also worth noting that between them the first two waves of this motive use ten of the available twelve semitones (the notes A and B are missing), thereby almost guaranteeing an effect that will be free from any key relationship, either expressed or implied, and leaving the composer free to generate his own harmonic language from this large amount of linear material.

The long 'slide' which follows the frost waves and the rapid movement in the left hand are obviously related to the frost motive. Many of the same notes are used, but in a different pattern and with an altered rhythmic articulation. The notes F, D and G sharp appear to be particularly important here and form a close link between the two programmatic ideas.

We next come to 'The Celestial Railroad'. The awkward-looking rhythm resolves itself into a series of train-like patterns, but the note organization in the bass again turns our thoughts back to the frost waves. Now the F, D and G sharp are joined by the A sharp that followed them in the original frost motive.

Feathertop the scarecrow is the next section with the little demons dancing around his pipe bowl. The empty-sounding consecutive fourths in the right hand may suggest the scarecrow's obvious lack of thinking machinery and the oscillating effect could well represent him swaying with the wind. The interesting thing is that he too is related to the frost motive by sharing a number of its notes. A look at the first line on p. 23 shows that the F, D and G sharp are still grouped together, with the first and last notes of the group sounded simultaneously.

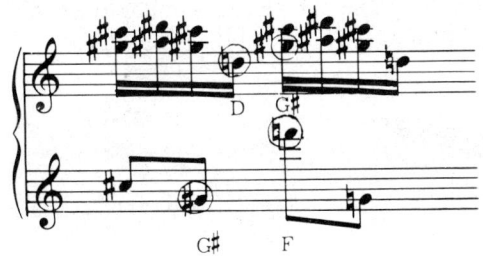

Then the boy 'jumps over the castle wall with Feathertop'. The basis of the frost motive is still present (D, G sharp and A sharp), although the F has now become an F sharp.

At this point we are able to observe something of the logic behind Ives' choice of notes, chords and patterns. In the programme, all these events are extensions of, and dependent on, the 'Magical Frost Waves'. In a similar manner, all the musical representation is also related to this same starting point.

With the section marked 'gradually slower' at the bottom of p. 24 we are in the old churchyard and the clusters on the next page have a rich, bell-like effect. The 'old hymn-tune that haunts the church and sings only to those in the churchyard' appears first on p. 32 (the 6/8 section) while the 'secular noises' drown it out before it has had a chance to get beyond the first note of its second phrase.

It reasserts itself on p. 33 (this time a semitone lower, and with greater effect), but it soon gives way to that moment 'when the circus parade comes down Main Street'. The material here comes from Ives' own *Country Band March* (1903) and contains all the usual clichés of the brass-band march: the strongly marked accents (with a few misses as some of the less expert members of the group miss their cues), the wrong notes that often appear mysteriously in performances by amateurs and all the stock melodic phrases and turns. The chords in the last line of p. 35 are the drum chords used by Ives in his childhood and there can be little doubt that the band 'take-off' owes much to his experiences in his father's village band.

The 'Slaves' Shuffle' is a quick ragtime movement, beginning on p. 36. The bass notes (marked with accent signs in the 1947 revision) show an interesting pattern:

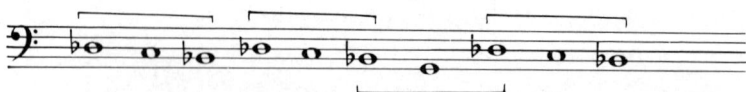

The descending note group finally plunges to the low G before starting again, so we could assume that the first and last notes of that group (the D flat and the B flat), together with the G, form the basis of the passage. If we put these three notes together we can see that they are all a minor third apart. If we then transpose the whole group a fifth higher we find that we have the vital notes from the frost motive — the F, D and G sharp — which were also separated by minor thirds. Thus we could look on the bass in the 'Slaves' Shuffle'.as a transposed version of our original group.

It may also, however, be regarded as an extension of that group. If we check back to the original statement of the frost motive we will see that the notes F, D and G sharp are followed by an A sharp. This note, enharmonically respelt as B flat, forms a common pivot point between the original motive and the version employed in the 'Slaves' Shuffle', making the latter a logical harmonic extension of the frost motive.

As well as having a programmatic validity, 'Hawthorne' can be seen as a scherzo with a purely musical structure. John Kirkpatrick describes it as seeming to be

> pure fantasy, the images following as if helter-skelter but actually in a symmetrical design: phantasmagoria — nocturne – ragtime – contrasts – ragtime – nocturne – phantasmagoria.[1]

This arch structure (compare Bartók) works as follows:

phantasmagoria	pp. 21–24
nocturne	pp. 24 (end)–26 (top)
ragtime	pp. 26–28
contrasts	pp. 28–35
ragtime	pp. 36–41 system 2
nocturne	pp. 41–42 top
phantasmagoria	pp. 42–50

The movement ends (or almost) with a small fragment marked 'slowly':

EXERCISE

Does this remind you of anything, in 'Hawthorne' or in the other movements?

DISCUSSION

If we look back at 'the old hymn tune that haunts the church and sings only to those in the churchyard to protect them from secular noises' we will see a very distinct relationship.

p.32   p.33   p.50

But there is much more to it than this. If we compare these phrases with the opening bars of 'The Alcotts', we will see that they are basically the same, binding the two movements together. Also, of course, they are closely related to the 'Beethoven' theme.

EXERCISE

What about the two sections we have neglected so far, pp. 26–32 and 41–50? Do you see there any thematic references to other parts of the Sonata?

DISCUSSION

p. 29 system 1, l.h.   'Beethoven'
p. 30 system 2 – p. 31 system 1, r.h.   'Sam Staples'
p. 31 system 2 – p. 32 system 1   'Beethoven'
p. 48 system 2 on   'Sam Staples'

---

1   Preface to Charles Ives, Symphony No. 4, Associated Music Publishers 1965, p. viii.

p. 49 systems 1–2 'Beethoven'

You may also have noticed on pp. 42–43 and 50 snatches of *Columbia Gem of the Ocean*, which, with a few switches of notes, can be seen as related to our motive [B] in 'Emerson':

EXERCISE

The music of 'Hawthorne' is certainly 'fantastic'. It is often wild, complex, dissonant; much of the material is not perhaps immediately attractive. Does this mean that it is not particularly good music?

DISCUSSION

I would argue that materials are often of less importance to a composer than the relationships, the inner meanings, he is able to establish. Perhaps, then, if the work sounds incomprehensible or unpleasant we are listening for the wrong things and missing the important points that the composer is making.

Ives' comments:

> Once a nice young man (his musical sense having been limited by three years' intensive study at the Boston Conservatory) said to Father, 'How can you stand it to hear old John Bell (the best stone mason in town) sing?' (as he used to at Camp Meetings). Father said, 'He is a supreme musician'. The young man (nice and educated) was horrified—'Why, he sings off the key, the wrong notes and everything—and that horrible, raucous voice—and he bellows out and hits notes no one else does—it's awful!' Father said, 'Watch him closely and reverently, look into his face and hear the music of the ages. Don't pay too much attention to the sounds—for if you do, you may miss the music. You won't get a wild, heroic ride to heaven on pretty little sounds.' [1]

1 *Memos*, p. 132.

My God! What has sound got to do with music! The waiter brings the only fresh egg he has, but the man at breakfast sends it back because it doesn't fit his eggcup.[1]

4.6 Fourth movement—'Thoreau'

In 1845 the naturalist and essayist Henry David Thoreau (1817–62) built himself a 'house' for $28 on Walden Pond, Concord, and lived there until September 1847. But it was not a hermit-like existence; he went into the town almost every day and his visitors were numerous. For his bare essentials (and they were few and simple) he would farm, build fences or survey (he was a trained surveyor) but he begrudged the time that had to be taken from what he regarded as his real business—studying and living with nature.

Thoreau's books were made up from notes scribbled in his journals and they are not always well organized. The style is a series of nervous, staccato bursts with sudden vivid turns of phrase and quite eloquent poetic passages at times, and although he was almost unknown as a writer in his lifetime his reputation is now equal to that of Emerson and Hawthorne, two of his Concord contemporaries. The fact that Ives rated Thoreau as highly as the other two writers is obvious and his placing of this movement at the end of the Sonata suggests that (in Ives' opinion) Thoreau might be a summary of all that Emerson, Hawthorne and the Alcotts represented, as well as being a fine example of 'the spirit of transcendentalism that is associated in the minds of many with Concord, Mass.'.

If Thoreau's writings can be adequately described as a collection of thoughts and ideas strung together, sometimes pedestrian and sometimes eloquently poetic, then this movement of the Sonata is a perfect mirror of the man and his thought processes. Every one of the ten pages presents us with a series of different rhythmic patterns, new melodic ideas (often of a fragmentary nature), changing chordal textures and musical reminiscences. At first glance it seems that here is a classic case of a piece of music that can only gain a sense of unity and purpose through the imposition of an extra-musical programme. In his *Essays Before a Sonata* Ives suggests that a programme may indeed exist, but, as you can see from the extract printed in the score, the sequence of events that he puts forward is as crowded and diverse as the musical styles contained in the movement itself.

Keeping this 'programme' in mind, let us examine the thematic material of the movement and see if there is any connection between the seemingly free ideas.

The first two chords, stated as arpeggios, show some very marked similarities in their construction. We have already noted Ives' interest in attempting to discover new chord formations and relationships (see above, Section 3.4) and here we have a practical demonstration. Chord 1 is the logical extension of the common practice of building chords from a series of superimposed thirds, but here (with the exception of one note of the series, which has been bypassed) Ives takes the system to its absolute limit. As the diagram shows, the addition of any further notes would bring us back to the beginning of the series again:

Chord 1: A C sharp E G B D sharp (F sharp) A sharp C sharp

The second chord uses the perfect fifth as its basic material with a small addition at the top of the range to make the chord a series of fifths plus a third.

Chord 2: E B F sharp C sharp G sharp D sharp (A C)

At the end of the second line on p. 62 we come to the first real thematic statement—perhaps this is the 'clearer thought, more traditional than the first'. For convenience we will label this as theme *A*.

1 Boatwright, p. 84.

Its importance can be judged by the fact that it is announced three times — the second on the last line of p. 62 and the third on the third line of p. 63 — though there are some small variations in these restatements. However, the essential 'skeleton' of the theme remains unaltered: the melody moves up a perfect fifth, D to A, sits around this upper note with the aid of the embellishing note G and then returns to its starting point.

In this emphasis on the perfect fifth we can see an immediate link with chord 2 at the start of the movement.

At the same time we should notice one particular feature of the bass line that supports theme *A* and its continuation (systems 2–4 of p. 62, for example). This bass descends from G to C, then fills in the scale from C to G before finally rising to C again.

The three most important notes are obviously the C, the G and the A — a combination that will be found frequently in the following bars.

The first subsequent appearance of this figure in fact occurs at the top of p. 64 in the left hand. The notes A, C and G form an ostinato figure which dominates most of the page. For the remainder of the analysis this figure will be referred to as theme *B*.

We can now see that this theme is only a contraction of the bass line that supported theme *A* and could, through its relationship with that theme, be related back to chord 2.

Over the top of the first statement of theme *B* we find another melodic fragment which is going to be heard several times in the course of the movement. This melody (the latter part of the first system on p. 64) will be called theme *C*:

As the above example shows, its underlying framework consists of four descending scale steps followed by a leap of a third in the same direction. We will find theme *C*

occurring again in the second and third systems of p. 64 and on the fourth and fifth systems of p. 67.

Soon another theme takes our attention. Theme *D*, basically a whole-tone melody, is first heard in the last line of p. 64. It also appears at the bottom of p. 66.

You may have noticed a certain similarity between themes *C* and *D*. Both begin with a descending pattern of four steps, and both then have a falling third:

It would therefore be quite possible to regard *D* as a further development of *C*.

The next interesting transformation occurs on p. 66, this time in the bass of the third and fourth systems.

EXERCISE

Look at the bass clusters in this passage (F–G–C–D) and see if you can relate them to any of the other themes in the movement.

DISCUSSION

The cluster (which we shall label as *E* for future reference) is made up of two superimposed sets of fifths: F–C and G–D. So immediately we may suspect that this is a very thinned-out restatement of chord 2, which was a compilation of fifths. You may also have seen it as a further development of the ostinato figure, theme *B*. If we transpose *B* to a higher pitch (beginning on D instead of A) we would have, as our transposed version of *B*, the notes D, F and C.

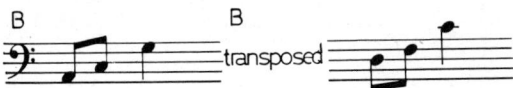

This figure already contains three of the four notes from the chord labelled *E*—the D, the F and the C. If this were to be extended by adding an extra fifth (quite a logical extension since it appears to be related to chord 2—which was a group of fifths—and since it contains the fifth as a vital part of its structure) we would have all the notes of chord *E* produced from a very simple development of the ostinato figure, *B*.

This extended figure could now be compressed into a chord:

47

But this chord is far too widely spaced for easy use, particularly when there are other notes to be played at the same time. It would therefore be more convenient if the placing of the essential notes were altered to suit the shape of the performer's hand. The result would probably look like this:

We can therefore see that chord *E* is doubly related to the opening of the movement, by its own intervallic content and by its construction as a development of theme *B* (which, you may remember, was drawn from the bass line of theme *A*, so *A*, *B* and *E* are all related).

There is only one more theme that we need to examine before taking stock of this complex web of melodic lines and chords. This new theme (which we shall designate *F*) appears in the middle of the third system of p. 67 (just before the third statement of theme *C*).

Again, you may have noticed its similarity to theme *C* (and therefore to theme *D*). All three commence with a descending scale passage followed by a drop of a third. However, now the number of stepwise notes has been reduced from four to three.

EXERCISE

Before we come to the flute entry on p. 69 let us pause to take stock. Write out an outline of the thematic relationships so far.

DISCUSSION

Themes *C*, *D* and *F* all begin the same way and so we could look on *D* and *F* as developments of *C*. The bass of theme *A* is condensed to form the ostinato figure *B* which, in its turn, is extended in a different direction to create chord E. Theme *A* we could relate to chord 2 by the use of the basic interval of a fifth.

This information could also be made into a table — a 'family tree' of themes.

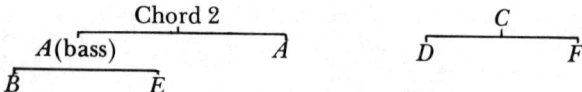

It would appear from this table that chord 1 was completely unnecessary and that themes *C*, *D* and *F* do not relate to the other material. However, an examination of this apparently 'left-over' material reveals that we have not been sufficiently thorough in our search for relationships. Chord 1 was a compilation of thirds; themes *C*, *D* and *F* also rely heavily on this interval, as the following example shows:

We can now see that these three themes are probably linear versions of chord 1.

However, it still appears that we have a dual structure. Chord 1 has its related thematic material (themes *C, D* and *F*) and chord 2 has a second independent group of themes (*A, B* and *E*). But further study shows one final relationship, this time between chords 1 and 2. The interval of a fifth (the basis of chord 2) can be made by the super-imposition of two thirds (the basis of chord 1). In fact, the first four notes of the movement show us a simple demonstration of this fact. The third A–C sharp plus the third C sharp–E combine to make the fifth A–E, and this addition is then strengthened by the use of another fifth, E–B to make the pattern

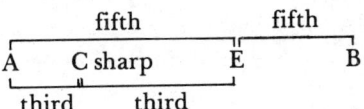

Chords 1 and 2 are further bound together by the use of common notes. Between them the two chords account for eleven of the twelve possible notes (D does not occur in either chord). Of these eleven notes, six are common to both chords. From these two pieces of evidence it would appear that we have before us a very ingeniously structured movement which could be shown in diagrammatic form as follows:

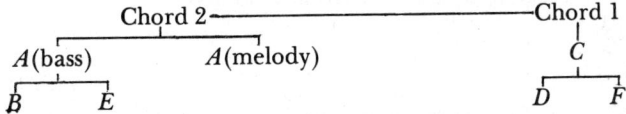

However, this final movement of the *Concord* Sonata still holds several surprises, and these are not revealed until p. 69. The first of these unexpected revelations is the need for a solo flute. Perhaps this can be justified by the programme: '. . . the poet's flute is heard out over the pond and Walden hears the swan song of that day . . .' The change in tone colour makes us very aware of the material that is being played at this vital moment.

EXERCISE

Can you identify the material?

DISCUSSION

The flute plays first 'Sam Staples', then 'Beethoven'. Key and mood both suggest it is 'The Alcotts' that is being recalled, and a direct quotation, p. 69 system 3 (compare p. 55 systems 1–2), confirms this. Notice though that the bass here consists of theme *B*.

At the end of the top system on p. 70 the flute seems about to play the 'Beethoven' theme again, but stops after only three Ds. Instead of the expected B flat we are given two statements by the piano of theme *F* (which of course also implies themes *C* and *D*, together with chord 1, as we have seen). This is followed by theme *C* itself as if to cement firmly the relationship between the two melodic phrases. The last system of the sonata begins by giving us chord 1 again followed quickly by the ostinato motive (theme *B*), together with a repeated chord figure in the r.h., which suggests the 'Beethoven' theme. However, this time the last note remains stationary instead of falling, as if a point of rest has been reached at last. But the cadence itself sounds far from final. Perhaps we are intended to let the Sonata sound on and grow in our imaginations.

EXERCISE

This last section is obviously a coda which aims to present a summary of all that has gone before. Why then does it only recapitulate some of the features from this last movement and the previous ones? Why not recall everything? Go over all the themes in the Sonata and try hard to think of an answer to this.

DISCUSSION

The amount of material from the final movement that is recapitulated is small, but small things are usually enough to jog a person's memory. Ives recalls the related themes *F* and *C*, thereby reminding us of their relationship to each other and to theme *D*. There is therefore no real need to recapitulate this latter melody. We also noticed that he used the ostinato figure (theme *B*). A quick check of the diagram showing the family tree of this movement will demonstrate that Ives has now reminded us not only of theme *B*, but also of the related themes *E* and *A*. His final statement of chord 1 will (he hopes) serve as a recapitulation for chord 2 also.

With reference to the other movements, the situation is similar. Ives quotes the 'Beethoven' theme from 'The Alcotts', but we have already seen (p. 43 above) that the 'old hymn' in 'Hawthorne' is related to this, and so we are reminded of that too. In fact, as Wiley Hitchcock points out, Ives is deliberately associating the Beethoven idea with two actual hymn tunes, *Missionary Chant* and *Martyn* (virtually quoted in 'The Alcotts' and 'Hawthorne' respectively).[1]

Since 'Beethoven' crops up in its 'pure' form also in 'Hawthorne', and in addition in 'Emerson', all the movements are being recalled. But we can go much further. 'Beethoven' is based on a falling third. The 'frost' motive from 'Hawthorne' (and the other themes in that movement derived from it) is built from thirds too, and so we are reminded of them also.

Turning to 'Sam Staples', also quoted in the coda to 'Thoreau', similarly striking connections are revealed. If we reverse the note-order in the upbeat, we have some-

1   Hitchcock, *Ives*, pp. 55–56.

thing very similar to 'Emerson' [A]. In addition themes *C*, *D* and *F* from 'Thoreau' are related as well. We can even tie in 'Emerson' [B] for, like the others, this consists basically of a descending scale.

The whole sonata, then, seems to be built out of two ideas. Ives himself suggests this in the essay on 'The Alcotts':

> All around you, under the Concord sky, there still floats the influence of that human faith melody [he means 'Sam Staples'], transcendent and sentimental enough for the enthusiast or the cynic respectively, reflecting an innate hope—a common interest in common things and common men—a tune the Concord bards are ever playing, while they pound away at the immensities with a Beethovenlike sublimity . . .

However, even this formulation is too divisive. We have already seen, in our discussion of 'The Alcotts', that the two themes are related through rhythmic similarity. There are also connections in pitch structure. 'Beethoven' consists of descending thirds arranged in a descending scale pattern. The 'human-faith melody' group also combines a descending third and a scale.

The final section of 'Thoreau' is therefore a true conclusion to the Sonata. It shows that the musical essence is the same for all four movements and at the same time it reminds us of the thematic transformations and developments that have taken place. Perhaps it also reminds us that Emerson, Hawthorne, the Alcotts and Thoreau were (at least in Ives' opinion) all of one spirit—that 'spirit of transcendentalism'.

Ives' comments:

The unity of a sonata movement has long been associated with its form, and to a greater extent than is necessary . . . Mr Richter or Mr Parker may tell us that all this is natural, for it is based on the classic-song form; but inspite of your teachers a vague feeling sometimes creeps over you that the form-nature of the song has been stretched out into deformity. Some claim for Tchaikovsky that his clarity and coherence of design is unparalleled (or some such word) in works for the orchestra. That depends, it seems to us, on how far repetition is an essential part of clarity and coherence. We know that butter comes from cream — but how long must we watch the 'churning arm'! If nature is not enthusiastic about explanation, why should Tchaikovsky be? . . . To Emerson, unity and the over soul, or the common-heart, are synonymous. Unity is at least nearer to these than to solid geometry, though geometry be all unity.[1]

---

1   Boatwright, p. 99.

5 Must a song always be a song?—'General William Booth enters into Heaven'

> After Father's death, Dr. Griggs . . . was the only musician friend of mine that showed any interest, toleration, or tried to understand the way I felt . . . about some things in music . . . A characteristic remark of his, that I remember, in speaking of the song, *General Booth* (which I played for him shortly after it was written in 1914 or so) was: 'It's a good song—but not a song'.[1]

The same may be said of many of Ives' compositions for voice and piano or voice and other instruments—they are not what singers and musicians of that period would have regarded as performable music and certainly not 'songs'. But is it necessary for a creative artist to keep within well-worn boundaries and by so doing perhaps to limit his artistic vision? Ives was convinced that it was not only unnecessary but ill-advised. Convention said that a work for voice and piano was a 'song', but must a composition that accepts the outward label of 'song' also accept the inner structure of works by other composers in a similar medium? In the 'Postface' to his *114 Songs* Ives wrote:

> Some of the songs in this book, particularly among the later ones, cannot be sung, and if they could, perhaps might prefer, if they had a say, to remain as they are; that is, 'in the leaf'—and that they will remain in this peaceful state is more than presumable. An excuse . . . for their existence which suggests itself at this point is that a song has a *few* rights, the same as other ordinary citizens . . . If it happens to feel like trying to fly where humans cannot fly, to sing what cannot be sung, to walk in a cave on all fours, or to tighten up its girth in blind hope and faith and try to scale mountains that are not, who shall stop it?—In short, must a song always be a song![2]

In other words, the medium must not be confused with the content. Bearing this in mind, let us now examine 'General William Booth enters into Heaven'. *Listen to the recording (Record 8, side 2 band 1) a few times before reading further.*

This song, on parts of a poem by Vachel Lindsay, is one of Ives' longest and most powerful. The strange mixture of effects and melodic quotations, combined with the fanatic, militaristic atmosphere of the text, gives us a very hectic picture of the first commander of the Salvation Army marching (perhaps almost storming) into heaven. The text is full of musical ideas and suggestions and Ives has built his material around these in an attempt to add an extra dimension to the poem. His melodic line, although at times seemingly awkward to sing, gives a very particular articulation to the text and his rhythmic patterns generally serve to carry the words along with a near speech rhythm.

In our discussion of 'General Booth' I would like to concentrate on Ives' use of word painting and quotation. Much of the song is march-like; indeed it begins with a typical brass-band drum beat—the snare drum (played by the right hand of the piano part) followed by the thud of the bass drum lagging a little behind the beat—no doubt a common feature of George Ives' band performances. In these opening bars we can see the 'drum' chords that were devised by Ives when he was a boy and practising drum parts on the piano.[3]

---

1 *Memos*, p. 116.
2 Boatwright, pp. 130–31.
3 '[I] got to trying out sets of notes to go with or take-off the drums . . . A popular chord in the right hand was . . . one with two white notes with the thumb, having the little finger run into a 7th or octave-and-semitone over the lower thumb note.' (*Memos*, pp. 42–43.)

This type of sonority pervades a great deal of the song. The second line of the poem quotes (in brackets) a line from a Salvation Army hymn — 'Are you washed in the blood of the Lamb?' — and Ives follows this example in the music. However, instead of quoting the Salvation Army tune he adds an extra dimension to the statement by using a tune derived from Lowell Mason's hymn *Cleansing Fountain* ('There is a fountain filled with blood').

EXERCISE

As I said, Lindsay places this line of text in brackets. What musical technique does Ives use to help parenthesize it?

DISCUSSION

He puts it in a different tonality from that of its musical context. The song starts in a kind of B minor/D major, but for the hymn quotation jumps to C major.

The poem often makes use of quotations from this hymn and each time Ives follows the pattern, but *his* quotations are given types of presentation to suit the poetic context.

EXERCISE

List the places where the hymn tune appears and briefly describe how it is presented and why (look at the text).

DISCUSSION

1 Bars 15–19 A parenthesis, therefore, like the first appearance, in a contrasting tonality (this time E major).

2 Bars 34–38 Again a parenthesis, but, perhaps because of the increased intensity of the text in the bars leading up to it ('Drabs . . . drug fiends . . . minds still passion ridden . . . vermin-eaten saints . . . unwashed legions . . .'), the tune is given a polytonal accompaniment. The chords contain three layers: an A natural bass, an F sharp seventh and a chord of C sharp.

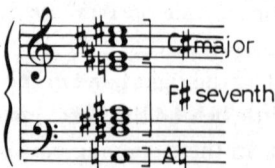

3 Bars 57–65 In keeping with the excitement here ('tranced fanatical they shrieked and sang'), the tune is given a fragmentary, rhythmically thrusting treatment, with syncopation and cross rhythms.

4 Bars 75–81 A parenthesis, so in a contrasting tonality (E flat). But this is a moment of climax ('on, on, upward thro' the golden air'), and Ives gives it a turbulent, 'muddy' accompaniment. However, the noise then fades away as a preparation for the next section.

5   Bars 82–91   The tune appears in the 'tenor' part of the piano accompaniment, though somewhat altered rhythmically. The mood is now tender and peaceful, to fit the words 'Jesus came to the courthouse door . . .', and the hymn winds its way through the texture, oscillating round the same few notes and rhythmically at odds with the rest of the music, in an obvious attempt to represent Booth, unaware of Jesus, leading his line of 'queer ones' round and round the Square.

6   Bars 97–105   The first complete statement of the hymn tune, 'spotless, clad in raiment new', in a broad, triumphant C major.

7   Bars 106–110   The tune is given a harmonization made up of chords drawn from the harmonic series (see Section 3.5 above), then a 'textbook' E major setting. The justification for this haunting ending, I think, is to add an extra emotional dimension to the text, to illuminate the seemingly simplistic climax we have just heard and make it 'real'. The healing completed, the fading drumbeats take the marching throng away.

There are other 'programmatic' elements in 'General Booth' too. In bar 52*ff*, when the text speaks of the way in which the 'Big voiced lassies made their banjos bang', the piano introduces the beginning of James A. Bland's minstrel-show song *Golden Slippers*, a relationship obviously prompted by the word 'banjo'.

In a similar manner the mention of trumpets in bars 70–73 ('Loons with trumpets blowed a blare') prompts Ives to use the bugle-call *Reveille* in the vocal part, accompanied by chordal fanfare figures on the piano.

EXERCISE

Do you think that Ives' 'programmatic' approach is a valid way of composing a song?

DISCUSSION

A part of the composer's aim is to give a greater insight into the text. If he can add nothing to the printed word then he might as well save himself (and us) the time and trouble. In other words, he should add an extra dimension to the written word. Ives' uses of quotation and pictorialism are employed to show us certain relationships that are (in his opinion) present in the text, just as his repetition of certain words serves to underline their importance for him. By these means he is separating what he considers to be the important points (the substance) from the vehicle that carries them (the manner) and is thus presenting us with both the original text and his own (simultaneous) commentary.

Ives' comments:

> Human attributes are definite enough when it comes to their description, but the expression of them or the paralleling of them in an art-process has to be . . . more or less arbitrary. But we believe that their expression can be less vague if the basic distinction of this art-dualism is kept in mind . . . [We will] assume that the higher and more important value of this dualism is composed of what may be called reality, quality, spirit, or substance against the lower value of form, quantity, or manner. Of these terms, 'substance' seems to us the most appropriate, cogent, and comprehensive for the higher, and 'manner' for the under-value.[1]

1   Boatwright, p. 75.

At any rate, we are going to be arbitrary enough to claim, with no definite qualification, that substance can be expressed in music, and that it is the only valuable thing in it; and, moreover, that in two separate pieces of music in which the notes are almost identical, one can be of substance with little manner and the other can be of manner with little substance. Substance has something to do with character. Manner has nothing to do with it.[1]

As well as being good illustrative material for Ives' use of quotation and programme (and also, in my view, a very fine song), 'General Booth' contains examples of most of the composer's favourite musical techniques—in chord construction and tonality, but above all, perhaps, in rhythm.

EXERCISE

A study of rhythm in this song would pay great dividends, and to get you on your way, look at the following passages and try to describe the rhythmic structure in each case: 1 bars 39–46; 2 bars 55–65; 3 bars 78–81; 4 bars 85–91.

DISCUSSION

1 The ♩♪ figure in the piano, as Ives' accent signs make clear, is accented on the *half* beat, so it conflicts with the accenting of the vocal line. In addition the vocal part seems to demand accents on the off beats (second and fourth rather than first and third). (Of course this passage is also a good example of bitonality. F major and D major triads are continually thrown against each other in the piano part.)

2 At first (bars 55–57) a piano part in 3/8 is put against an irregularly accented vocal line. When the voice becomes more regular (bars 58–60, basically 4/4), the piano l.h. retains a 3/8 pattern. From bar 61 to 65 voice and piano are together and the interesting point is the use of irregular metre: 7/8 (= 3/4 + 1/8) then 4/4 then 7/8 then 4/4.

3 Regular semiquaver patterns on the piano are placed against a vocal line of total rhythmic irregularity, its divisions of the crotchet unit being quite complex. On the whole the rhythmic values in the vocal part gradually lengthen, thus helping to slow down the music.

4 We have already seen that the hymn tune in the 'tenor' area is rhythmically at odds with the rest of the music. In addition, Ives portrays the 'round and round' idea by means of a three-note circling motive in the voice and an oscillating two-note figure in the piano r.h. The three-note motive is in 3/4 while the r.h. figure is in 2/4. From bar 89 on the voice's 3/4 is 'stretched' in a similar way to bars 79–81; irregular divisions, against the piano's regular crotchet, create marvellous representation of never-ending movement.

1 Boatwright, p. 77.

6 The Fourth Symphony

Ives' Fourth Symphony is the densest and most complex of his completed orchestral works (though the unfinished *Universe Symphony* would have surpassed it). Simply understanding the score can prove baffling even to experienced musicians, and it is worth noting that the first complete performance was not given until as recently as 1965. In a study such as this, with limitations on time and money, to deal with this work at anything more than a very superficial level is almost impossible.

Why, then, is it included at all? Partly because we have not yet examined any of the features of Ives' orchestral writing and partly because, as one of his largest works, it at least deserves some comment. The main reason for its inclusion, however, is because the Fourth Symphony is one of Ives' most comprehensive compositions, embracing nearly all the styles and techniques of his earlier smaller works in one huge virtuosic sweep. A summary such as this work presents cannot lightly be ignored.

Officially the symphony was composed between 1909 and 1916, but actually some of the movements — or at least sections of some movements — were completed much earlier and merely incorporated into the Fourth Symphony. In fact no fewer than

Autograph score of Ives' Fourth Symphony, second movement

fifteen previous pieces contributed material to the symphony. A study of the content of each of the four movements is a study of Ives' notebooks, sketches and ideas of a lifetime, for the work is crowded with musical reminiscences, quotations and inspirations, both good and bad. It is a summary of acoustical theories and experiments, some of which even date back to Ives' childhood when he followed his father's (often eccentric) tests and demonstrations. We hear examples of most of the technical features mentioned above in Section 3, together with a number of other devices that can only be described as typical of Ives. But above all, despite this borrowing of material (from himself and from other composers), this restatement of old ideas and this series of experiments, we hear a rare originality and freshness. The term 'symphony' takes on a new dimension in Ives' hands.

Ives' comments:

> . . . I was getting somewhat tired of hearing the lily boys say, 'This a symphony? — Mercy! — Where is the first theme of twelve measures in C major? — Where are the next 48 measures of nice (right kind of) development leading nicely into the second theme in G? (second Donkey contrasting with Ass 1) — the nice German recipe etc. — give it a ride, Arthur! — to hell with it! — Symphony 'with sounds' — my Symphony![1]

> Some nice people, whenever they hear the words 'Gospel Hymns' . . . say 'Mercy Me!', and a little high-brow smile creeps over their brow — 'Can't you get something better than that in a symphony?' The same nice people, when they go to a properly dressed symphony concert under proper auspices, led by a name with foreign hair, and hear Dvořák's *New World Symphony*, in which they are told this famous passage was from a negro spiritual, then think it must be quite proper, even artistic, and say 'How delightful!' But when someone proves to them that the Gospel Hymns are fundamentally responsible for the negro spirituals, they say 'Ain't it awful!' . . .[2]

Like most of Ives' instrumental works, the Fourth Symphony is programmatic. For a performance of two movements in 1927 notes were written by his friend Henry Bellamann, no doubt from information supplied by the composer:

> This symphony . . . consists of four movements, — a prelude, a majestic fugue, a third movement in comedy vein, and a finale of transcendent spiritual content. [The order of the second and third movements was later reversed.] The aesthetic program of the work is . . . the searching questions of what? and why? which the spirit of man asks of life. This is particularly the sense of the prelude. The three succeeding movements are the diverse answers in which existence replies . . . The fugue . . . is an expression of the reaction of life into formalism and ritualism. The succeeding movement [now the second] . . . is a comedy in the sense that Hawthorne's Celestial Railroad is a comedy.'

Ives himself added, 'The last movement is an apotheosis of the preceding content, in terms that have something to do with the reality of existence and its religious experience.'[3]

Radio programme 12 is devoted to Ives' Fourth Symphony, and you will be able to hear substantial parts of the music then. The following notes are intended to provide general background to the work and you should read them before listening to the programme.

1 *Memos*, p. 94.
2 *Memos*, p. 52.
3 Quoted in John Kirkpatrick's preface to Ives' Symphony No. 4, p. viii.

First movement

Almost all the material of this movement originally appeared in the First Violin Sonata of 1907 (before that it came from a setting of *Watchman tell us of the Night* for soprano and organ dating from 1901) and subsequently it went through various versions, including a song for voice and piano of 1913, before finding its place at the start of the Fourth Symphony. It is the shortest of the four movements and in it Ives indulges in one of his favourite compositional techniques—the extension of a hymn melody. The tune is one of his oft-quoted favourites: Lowell Mason's *Watchman tell us of the Night*:

A strong orchestral opening gradually dies away as the choir sings two verses of this somewhat contemplative melody, accompanied by quietly moving (but nevertheless strong and often dissonant) harmonies and some intricate cross rhythms produced by the interaction of the chorus and orchestra. Fragments of other hymn tunes are woven into this orchestral texture.

The setting given to *Watchman* may perhaps give us some idea of the type of harmonization that Ives favoured for hymn tunes. His dissonances are not merely employed as effects, nor are they used to highlight emotive words or phrases. Instead they are merely logical extensions of the basic chords themselves (this technique was discussed above in Section 3.1). However, it is unlikely that Ives made excessive use of this style of writing during his period as a church organist since he felt that the treatment of 'religious' themes in this symphony was his freest and most natural.

Second movement

The second movement is drawn partly from the 'Hawthorne' movement of the *Concord* Sonata. Hawthorne's story, *The Celestial Railroad*, provides the programme:

> . . . an exciting, easy and worldly progress through life is contrasted with the trials of the Pilgrims in their journey through the swamp. The occasional slow episodes—Pilgrims' hymns—are constantly crowded out and overwhelmed by the former. The dream, or fantasy, ends with an interruption of reality—the Fourth of July in Concord—brass band, drum corps, etc. . . . .[1]

A rhythmically complicated introduction begins the movement. Two conductors are required, the first conductor controlling the main body of the orchestra at one tempo (Allegretto, ♩. of 6/8 = 50) and the second conductor being responsible for the lower voices (bassoons in 7/4 time, ♩ = 70 and basses playing unbarred music, ♩ = 80). As we have observed, this concept of polyrhythmic multi-layered music is at the heart of Ives' style.

A brief quiet section using quarter-tone string chords follows, and then a suggestion, on two solo violins, of the hymn tune *God be with you till we meet again*.

Suddenly the lower strings, timpani and solo piano begin a new rhythmic pattern—we are once again on the Celestial Railroad! The train slowly gathers speed as it sounds four short, sharp blasts on its whistle—an extremely realistic effect produced by the upper woodwinds.

---

1 Quoted in Kirkpatrick, *op. cit.*, p. viii.

As the movement progresses there are many bars requiring two independent conductors to control the complexities of this intensely active music. At times ostinato figures emerge, contrasting with the main orchestral sound. Fragments of many hymns and popular tunes are worked in, among them *In the Sweet By and By*, *Columbia Gem of the Ocean*, *Beulah Land*, *Yankee Doodle*, *Marching through Georgia* and *Turkey in the Straw*. Quiet sections ('Pilgrims' hymns') are contrasted with outbursts of 'secular noises'. The climax ('Fourth of July in Concord') is based on the brass-band take off from Ives' own *Country Band March*, and after this the movement quickly subsides to a close. The Celestrial Railroad does not run down or come to a standstill; instead the train passes swiftly from our audible 'view' and disappears into the distance almost in mid-phrase.

Third movement

The four movements of Ives' first string quartet (?1898) are labelled 'Chorale'–'Prelude'–'Offertory'–'Postlude'. The first movement derives from an earlier fugue written for Horatio Parker (probably in 1897, for organ). In 1909 the quartet was revised and the first movement omitted. This first movement was also revised and scored for orchestra, and became the third movement of the Fourth Symphony. Very few of the actual notes were changed during the revision process; the main rewriting was concerned with the disposition of the quartet parts within the orchestra and with a search for the greater clarity that is available through the use of a wider and more varied range of timbres.

The form of this movement is outwardly that of a fugue, but the internal organization is quite unlike the pattern used by Bach for this form and equally unlike the fugal writing employed by other composers of Ives' generation. The subject is the hymn tune *Missionary* ('From Greenland's icy mountains') by Lowell Mason:

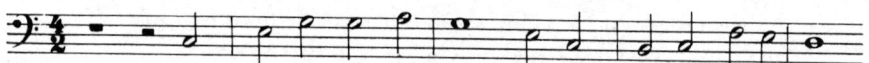

However, a second subject is soon introduced by the horn:

This derives from another hymn tune, Oliver Holden's *Coronation* ('All hail the power of Jesus' name'), and, although it is at first used as a counter subject (appearing only as a support to statements of the subject or its answer), the new melody soon frees itself from this function and becomes almost as important as the subject itself. The result is therefore more of a fugue on two subjects than a fugue with a regular counter subject.

Some writers have suggested that it is rather odd for Ives to adopt the fugal form with its regular procedures and carefully defined patterns, and that forms such as canon, fugue and strict imitation have all proved unsatisfactory in his hands. Even Henry Cowell (normally Ives' staunchest defender) suggests that, in this movement of the Fourth Symphony

. . . the music seems far too cramped, as though he did not really wish to stay within the confines of a fugue, but was for some reason forced to keep his wings tied. One misses the freedom of fancy. [1]

If there is any cramped formality in the movement it may perhaps be due to the fact that it was an early work, written while Ives was still a student at Yale. However, had he felt that the work was unsuitable in its present state he would almost certainly have recast it during the 1909 revision. Clearly, then, its inclusion is a deliberate choice arousing out of the needs of the symphony's programme ('. . . the reaction of life into formalism and ritualism').

Fourth movement

The finale begins softly: a battery of percussion instruments (snare drum, medium drum, bass drum, cymbals and gong) under the direction of a separate conductor play the first eight bars *ad libitum*. They then settle down to a carefully notated tempo, and throughout the movement this group sticks to its own rhythmic pattern and its own tempo, whatever the rest of the orchestra is doing. The result is a series of rhythmic tensions, climaxes and releases, all carefully controlled by Ives and caused by the differing speed and duration relationships set up between the two groups. At times their patterns, if not actually similar, are complementary, and the feeling of instability or tension is small. But at other times the rhythms are violently contrasted, thereby setting up enormous tension. Ives also makes use of gradations between these two extremes, allowing tension to build gradually at some points or having it mount rapidly at others. This twin-group relationship exists throughout the movement and is only silenced at the final cadence when the small percussion ensemble play their last notes, the main orchestral body having faded away several bars before.

After the quiet, unpitched opening the bass instruments slowly form the notes of a melodic line (the hymn tune *Bethany* — 'Nearer my God to Thee') almost as if they were searching laboriously for each sound. This melody, on which the whole movement is based, is short-lived, however, and soon complex chord patterns begin to form as the movement slowly gathers momentum.

Other melodic fragments emerge from the richly textured background. Many of these are not original melodies; Ives is indulging in one of his favourite pastimes, the quotation of musically altered popular melodic fragments. However, without a thorough study of the score any attempt to play 'spot the tune' is usually fruitless as Ives has skilfully adjusted and varied his raw material. It becomes virtually a composer's commentary on the basic material rather than a series of direct quotations — a development of ideas rather than a collage of cutouts.

The relationships of the various orchestral forces Ives uses is extremely intricate. He calls for a large orchestra including orchestral and solo pianos, an organ, a 'distant choir' of a few strings and harp, the independent percussion battery, and a choir. The choir enters for the coda, which provides a thrilling conclusion to the whole symphony. While the orchestra play extremely softly and delicately the women's voices, wordless, begin a long and drawn out version of *Bethany*,

This melody soon ceases, however, and the chorus resumes in five- and six-part harmonies with each voice oscillating around the last notes of the hymn while the orchestral sound supporting them grows gradually softer. Finally even the choir fades into silence, leaving only the percussion group to end the movement as it began.

1 Cowell, *op. cit.*, p. 151.

7 The place of Ives in twentieth-century music

How should we evaluate the place and importance of Ives in twentieth-century music — his particular role in the rise of so-called 'modernism'? Perhaps the question may even be phrased as 'Is Ives a great composer?', or 'What makes a great composer?'

When this latter question was put to a class of teenage boys some years ago the answers were enlightening, and ranged from 'He has to be someone who has written LOTS of music' through 'Someone that everyone has heard about' to 'He's got to be dead!'. When judged by these criteria Ives is certainly a great composer. His own catalogue lists over 100 titles (many, such as *A Book of 114 Songs*, covering a number of smaller works) while Henry Cowell[1] lists 164 vocal and choral works and 49 instrumental pieces that had been published by 1968, without even mentioning the vast collection of music still in manuscript. With regard to reputation, Cowell assures us that 'Today the music of Charles Ives has a much wider audience in the United States than that of the other three major composers of the first half of the twentieth century.'[2] (However he neglects to tell us who 'the other three major composers' were.) On the final point, Ives died on 19 May 1954.

Obviously there is much more to finding an answer to our question than this and perhaps some of this gap may be filled by looking at Ives in an historical perspective. By doing this we may be able to examine his part in the shaping of new styles — in short, to examine his 'influence'.

Our study so far has given us a glimpse of music in America before Ives and it has given us some idea of the path that he could have followed if he wished — a continuation of the tradition that he had inherited from his teachers and from his musical environment. The fact that he chose to depart from these conventions may suggest either that he was incapable of handling them or that he saw the old style as coming to a dead end and wished to find alternative ways of writing.

The first suggestion — that Ives was technically unable to write 'conventional' tonal music — can be discarded at once since we have a considerable body of evidence to prove the contrary. His examination results from Yale, for example, show that, although Ives was not a brilliant composition student, he was at least a competent craftsman. Similarly, his record as a church organist suggests that he was a very capable performer: the programmes of some of his early recitals (given when he was only 14 or 15 years of age) include works demanding quite a high standard of executive ability. While this evidence may, on the one hand, only indicate that he had a high degree of manual dexterity, it may, on the other hand, suggest that he knew the traditional repertoire well and had learned from it. Either way, it is obvious from his music, writings and general behaviour that Ives completely rejected the traditional style in favour of his own highly personal idiom, and that this rejection was a matter of choice rather than necessity.

It would therefore appear that Ives' importance as a composer hinges on this personal style. We have already examined many aspects of it and seen how it evolved — by a series of experiments and studies, and by sheer hard work in (musically) isolated surroundings. By his experiments Ives proved, for instance, that to build chords out of a series of thirds was not the only method of chord construction; other intervals and even quarter tones were equally well suited to form the basis of a viable harmonic system. This proof was then extended further to show that microtonal intervals may be incorporated into melodic lines since these melodies are often harmonically conceived.

1 Cowell, *op. cit.*
2 Cowell, *op. cit.*, p. 207.

In a similar way Ives showed that music need not always be rhythmically tied to a constant metrical pulse. As we saw in the *Concord* Sonata, he demonstrated how notes may be related to each other in their duration without the constantly present pulse and bar line to act as a clock that pounds out the common rhythmic denominator. Throughout his work he used complex polyrhythmic devices, and, in the last movement of the Fourth Symphony, he showed how a metrical pulse may be used to create (instead of just heighten) a climax, making it possible to have rhythmic and melodic-harmonic climaxes and releases at different points. Techniques such as these helped to free composers from the 'straitjacket' imposed on them by the use of conventionally notated rhythms with their limited number of patterns and combinations.

Melodically, Ives took great steps forward although very few of his melodies are singable or even particularly memorable. His contribution was to explode the myth that melody is the basis of all music by simply combining vast numbers of melodies and fragments in different styles, forms and keys. The result is not so much melodic music as *texture* music. In some abstract paintings the individual lines are so merged that they present not a single series of recognizable outlines but a collection of differing densities and textures. The artist has made up his picture by balancing, contrasting and relating these different textures to each other and the result can be a unified and coherent whole. In music, Ives followed a similar path. His brief melodic quotations (as we saw in the Fourth Symphony) do not appear as individual lines, but rather as part of an overall texture, and although we may not be able to point to the first and second subjects of a movement, we are made aware of the fact that it is divided into a number of sub-sections by the use of varying orchestral colours, textures and densities. If we add to this such devices as the neo-serial techniques that Ives often used and such innovations as the multiple tempo writing of the Fourth Symphony, it is clear that he made a great contribution in the area of musical form. We can thus confidently say that Ives made vast changes in all of the five basic elements of music: melody, harmony, rhythm, form and texture. These changes were larger and more radical in some pieces than in others, but overall it is an impressive achievement, especially since it was carried through without knowledge of what the European modernists were doing and in many cases ahead of them. We can say then that Ives is an *important* composer in the twentieth century, even if this does not necessarily mean that he is a 'great' composer.

If we are searching for a 'great' composer, one who has enormous influence on the course of musical history, there is one point that is certainly not in Ives' favour, although how much of it was his fault and how much was the fault of American musicians, audiences and critics is hard to decide. This is the fact that Ives' discoveries, achievements and technical advances were conceived and carried through in musical isolation. Ives taught no other composers, nor did he found any group of followers or imitators[1]; all that he did was for his own satisfaction. Although he virtually ceased composing in the 1920s, very little of his work was known for the next thirty years. During this time several other composers independently evolved similar techniques and a number of other alternatives to tonality became available. It is interesting to speculate on what course music might have taken in this century if the work of Charles Ives had been well known in the 1920s, 30s and 40s, but the plain truth is that it was not known and the efforts of other composers proved to be of far greater influence on twentieth-century European music. Actually, despite his innovations, Ives' 'neo-romantic' traits—his programmatic tendency, his idealism, his expressiveness, his open-endedness—would not, I think, have commended him to the 1920s and 30s (basically a neoclassical period), and his real discovery had to await the looser, more experimental scene of the 1960s.

1 Though a short-lived group of young Americans—the Young Composers Group, including Bernard Herrmann, Jerome Moross and Lehmann Engel—did adopt Ives as a figurehead in the early 1930s.

There is no doubt that Ives is a fascinating composer and a great milestone in American musical history: he is certainly the first great American composer and possibly the best that country has yet produced. Unfortunately he is too often labelled as merely an 'interesting' composer. Although his lack of immediate influence precluded the possibility of his changing the shape of early twentieth-century musical history, as Schoenberg and Stravinsky could claim to have done, his achievements provide a significant gloss on the important developments, a reinforcement and a highly personal expansion of them, which to later composers like John Cage has come to seem indispensable.

8 List of the most important works of Ives

Most of Ives' works were not published in his lifetime. His manuscripts form a vast and chaotic collection, untidily written, with gaps where material has been lost. His compositional methods included continual revision and self-borrowing. For all these reasons the process of compiling a catalogue is formidable. Despite a great deal of work, notably by John Kirkpatrick, the task is still not complete. If you are interested, I would refer you to John Kirkpatrick, *A Temporary Mimeographed Catalogue of the Music Manuscripts and Related Materials of Charles Edward Ives*, Library of the School of Music, New Haven 1960.

The most important of Ives' works are probably these (dates of composition are from Kirkpatrick's catalogue):

Piano

Three-Page Sonata (1905)
Sonata No. 1 (1902–9)
Sonata No. 2, *Concord, Mass., 1840–1860* (1909–15)

Vocal

114 Songs (published 1922, available now in the form of various smaller collections)

Chamber

Sonata No. 1 for violin and piano (1903–8)
Sonata No. 2 for violin and piano (1903–10)
Sonata No. 3 for violin and piano (1902–14)
Sonata No. 4 for violin and piano, *Children's Day at the Camp Meeting* (1892–1906, 1914–15)
String Quartet No. 1, *A Revival Service* (1896)
String Quartet No. 2 (1907–13)

Small orchestra

Over the Pavements (1906–13)
Set for Theatre or Chamber Orchestra (1906–11)
The Unanswered Question (1906)
Central Park in the Dark (1906)

Orchestra

Symphony No. 1 (1895–8)
Symphony No. 2 (1896–1902)
Symphony No. 3, *The Camp Meeting* (1904–11)
Symphony No. 4 (1909–16)
New England Holidays (1904–13)
Orchestral Set No. 1, *Three Places in New England* (1903–14)
Orchestral Set No. 2 (1909–15)
Robert Browning Overture (1908–12)

Part 2: Varèse

9 Biographical details

9.1 The early years

Edgard Varèse was born on 22 December 1883 in Paris, the son of Henri Varèse, an engineer. His early childhood was spent in Paris and in Villars, a village in Burgundy, but in 1892 he moved with his family to Italy to live in Turin. During these years Varèse wished to study music but his father was against such frivolities and insisted that his son should study mathematics and physics. So great was this family antipathy to any form of musical study that the piano in the Varèse household was locked.

This, however, did not deter the young Varèse and he recalled in a conversation with the American composer Gunther Schuller[1] that at the age of eleven he wrote an opera based on Jules Verne's *Martin Paz*. Such activities brought Varèse to the notice of Giovanni Bolzoni, the Director of the Turin Conservatory, who took an interest in him and gave him private lessons. Despite this, Varèse was apparently not impressed with the materials of music. He commented to Schuller, 'I detested the piano and all conventional instruments, and when I first learned the scales my only reaction was, "Well they all sound alike".'[2]

Varèse grew to hate his father, who seems to have been violent as well as antagonistic to the idea of his son studying music, and in 1903 he decided to leave his family and to return to Paris for further musical studies. In 1904, living in 'bohemian poverty', he was admitted to the Schola Cantorum. Here he studied composition with d'Indy, fugue with Roussel and medieval and renaissance music with Charles Bordes. Roussel became a friend and Bordes' teaching gave rise to Varèse's life-long passion for early music. His comments on d'Indy, however, were impolite and he felt that he had learnt little from his teaching. (He was probably thinking of d'Indy when he remarked of professors that they were 'ruled like music paper'.) After only one year of this tuition Varèse left the Schola Cantorum and was admitted to the master classes of Charles Widor at the Paris Conservatoire. Widor, he felt, was an open-minded musician and a first-class organist. This respect did not extend to the Conservatoire itself, however, nor to the French musical thinking of the period. Varèse found himself limited by the traditional tonal system and the tempered tuning system, and he looked for some alternatives. His early mathematical and scientific training had left its mark; Varèse felt that in other subjects, such as chemistry or physics, the basic assumption was that there was always something to be discovered. Music, however, appeared to him to be a series of imposed systems, as if the final stages of musical development had been reached. Musical instruments, without any further modifications, were capable of giving a much wider range of sounds, yet music was strictly limited to the sounds of the tempered scale.

Varèse was earning his living by music copying, orchestrating and teaching, but he did have several minor successes in Paris during this period. In 1906 he started a choir at the Université Populaire du Faubourg Saint-Antoine, a people's university founded in 1899, and elsewhere at least one of his early works—a piano version of *Rhapsodie Romane*—was performed. In the following year, on the recommendation of Massenet and Widor, he was awarded the Première Bourse Artistique de la Ville de Paris en Musique (an award given every year by the municipality in music, architecture, painting and sculpture). However, he failed in the competition for the Prix de Rome in

1 Gunther Schuller, 'Conversation with Varèse', *Perspectives of New Music*, 3,2 (Spring-Summer 1965), p. 32.
2 Schuller, *op. cit.*, p. 32.

1906 and shortly after was expelled from the Conservatoire after an argument with Fauré. He had already composed quite an impressive list of orchestral works including *Trois Pièces*, *La Chanson des Jeunes Hommes*, *Le Prélude à la Fin d'un Jour* and *Rhapsodie Romane*. These scores are all lost, only one work from this period, the song 'Un Grand Sommeil Noir', surviving. Judging by this song, and comments on other pieces ('medieval spirit'[1], 'calm and religious character'[2], 'a profane Gregorian chant'[3]), Varèse's style at this time may have been marked by the use of 'organum-like progressions in a free contrapuntal texture that created a number of clashing dissonances'[4]. Such techniques could have originated both from his study of medieval music and from his enthusiasm for Debussy. Here is the opening of 'Un Grand Sommeil Noir':

However, Varèse disliked the musical life of Paris and, despite the promise his career was showing, he left for Berlin towards the end of 1907:

> I left Paris impelled by a disgust for all the petty politics there, searching for a way of escaping from myself, for a way of escaping from middle-class sentiment, that sentiment which neutralises the efforts and the sensibility of the most astute, the most intelligent of peoples, and of the French elite, the first in the world.[5]

9.2   Berlin

> In 1907 . . . I went to Berlin, where I spent most of the next seven years, and had the good fortune of becoming (in spite of the disparity of age and importance) the friend of Ferruccio Busoni, then at the height of his fame. I had read his remarkable little book, *A New Aesthetic of Music* (a milestone in my musical development), and when I came upon 'Music is born free; and to win freedom is its destiny,' it was like hearing the echo of my own thought.[6]

Busoni was a great help and encouragement to Varèse during these years; but he made many trips to Paris, and a list of his friends at the time, in Berlin, Paris and elsewhere, reads rather like a *Who's Who* of the arts in the first decades of this century, including Debussy, Satie, Richard Strauss and the Futurist Russolo (though Varèse was anti-Futurist), the sculptor Rodin, the artists Picasso, Modigliani, Léger, Derain and Dufy, and the writers Hugo von Hofmannsthal, Romain Rolland, Guillaume Apollinaire and Max Jacob. The single most important influence on him at this time was probably

1   Journalist on Varèse's compositions in *Courrier de Bayonne*, September 1905; quoted in Louise Varèse, *Varèse, A Looking-Glass Diary*, Vol. 1, Davis-Poynter 1973, p. 68.

2   Romain Rolland on *Bourgogne* (1908), letter to Varèse; quoted in Louise Varèse, *op. cit.*, p. 58.

3   Sâr Péladan on *Rhapsodie Romane*; quoted in Fernand Ouellette, *Edgard Varèse*, Calder and Boyars 1973, p. 19.

4   David Harold Cox, 'Stylistic Evolution in the Music of Edgard Varèse', *First American Music Conference*, Keele University, 1978, p. 102.

5   *Le Petit Marseillais*, 13 March 1932, quoted in Ouellette, *op. cit.*, p. 21.

6   Fernand Ouellette, *Visages d'Edgard Varèse*, Editions de l'Hexagone 1959, p. 10; quoted in translation in Louise Varèse, *op. cit.*, p. 49.

the ideas of Busoni—particularly on the need to extend the available musical material and break the straitjacket of the tempered scale, and to construct new, electronic instruments—but Debussy was important for his music too: his clarity and economy of material impressed Varèse as much as his 'balancing with almost mathematical equilibrium timbres against rhythms and textures—like a fantastic chemist'.[1] Sometimes he felt that Strauss had a similar clarity in his work, and he admired the use of silence in the works of both these composers.

In Berlin Varèse survived by music copying, teaching and conducting, and he also composed a number of new works. Through Strauss' influence, his orchestral work *Bourgogne* was performed in 1910; it was received with hostility. Unfortunately, like almost all his early music, the score was later destroyed, but Varèse has left us a brief description of his style and ideals at this time, phrased in his usual scientific manner:

> I was trying to approximate the kind of inner, microcosmic life you find in certain chemical solutions, or through the filtering of light . . . The earlier works were what I would call architectonic. I was working with blocks of sound, calculated and balanced against each other. I was preoccupied with volume in an architectural sense, and with projection . . . I wanted to find a way to project in music the concept of calculated or controlled gravitation, how one element pushing on the other stabilizes the total structure, thus using the material elements at the same time in opposition to and in support of one another. I think I would characterise my early music as granitic![2]

During the First World War Varèse served with the French Army. His general health, however, was not good and on this account he was discharged in 1915. Normal musical activities had, of course, been considerably disturbed by the war. Although music was still being performed in Europe the concerts themselves at times had heavy political or patriotic overtones; the works performed were drawn largely from the standard repertoire and there was little scope for a thirty-two-year-old conductor and composer who believed that musical materials required revitalizing. For this reason Varèse left Europe for America, arriving on 29 December 1915.

9.3   America

In New York his abilities, particularly as a conductor, soon found recognition and in 1919 he founded the New Symphony Orchestra. Its purpose was to perform new music, but the first concert was so badly received that the orchestra switched to more conservative programmes and Varèse resigned. Two years later, in an attempt to assist contemporary composers, he formed the International Composers' Guild, the first organization of its kind. The manifesto of July 1921 reads:

> The composer is the only one of the creators of today who is denied direct contact with the public. When his work is done he is thrust aside, and the interpreter enters, not to try to understand the composition but impertinently to judge it. Not finding in it any trace of the conventions to which he is accustomed, he banishes it from his programs, denouncing it as incoherent and unintelligible.

> In every other field, the creator comes into some form of direct contact with his public. The poet and novelist enjoy the medium of the printed page; the painter and sculptor, the open doors of the gallery; the dramatist, the free scope of a stage. The composer must depend upon an intermediary, the interpreter.

1   Schuller, *op. cit.*, p. 33.
2   Schuller, *op. cit.*, pp. 33–34.

It is true that in response to public demand, our official organizations occasionally place on their programs a new work surrounded by established names. But such a work is carefully chosen from the most timid and anemic of contemporary production, leaving absolutely unheard the composers who represent the true spirit of our time.

Dying is the privilege of the weary. The present day composers refuse to die. They have realized the necessity of banding together and fighting for the right of each individual to secure 'fair and free presentation of his work'. It is out of such collective will that the International Composers' Guild was born.

The aim of the International Composers' Guild is to centralize the works of the day, to group them in programs intelligently and organically constructed and, with the distinguished help of singers and instrumentalists to present these works in such a way as to reveal their fundamental spirit.

The International Composers' Guild refuses to admit any limitation, either of volition or of action.

The International Composers' Guild disapproves of all 'isms'; denies the existence of schools; recognizes only the individual.

The ICG lasted until 1927 and introduced many modern works, European and American, to New York audiences. In 1928 Varèse, together with two other composers, Henry Cowell and Carlos Chávez, founded the Pan American Association of Composers, to perform music by composers from the Americas. Nicolas Slonimsky was principal conductor and over the next few years he gave many PAAC concerts, in Europe as well as America.

As in Paris and Berlin, Varèse in New York was at the centre of avant-garde artistic activity. As well as Cowell and Chávez, his friends included the composer and harpist Carlos Salzedo, the composer and painter Carl Ruggles, the photographer Alfred Steiglitz and the artists Duchamp, Picabia and Stella.

In 1922 disaster seemed to overtake Varèse. He learned that all his pre-war manuscripts, which he had stored in a Berlin warehouse, had been destroyed by fire. Apart from the song mentioned earlier, the only evidence of any of his early works was the manuscript of *Bourgogne* (which he destroyed himself in 1960). His remaining (American) works were few: *Amériques* ('. . . the title . . . not purely geographic but . . . symbolic of discoveries—new worlds on earth, in the sky, or in the minds of men'[1]) and *Offrandes* had been completed and he was working on a new piece scored for two woodwinds, seven brasses and percussion, to be called *Hyperprism*. Varèse conducted its first performance in March 1923 at an International Composers' Guild Concert in New York—and provoked a riot in the audience. The sheer, physical wall of sound and the heavy block-like structures of *Hyperprism* had an unusual effect on its hearers. One critic spoke of 'two frantic camps one of which hissed, the other hissed the hissers'[2], and another reported that

> . . . it remained to Edgard Varèse . . . to cause peaceful lovers of music to scream in agony, to arouse angry emotions, and tempt men to retire to the back of the theatre and perform tympani concertos on each other's faces . . .[3]

This event, however, did not cause Varèse to stop composing and three new works (now among his most popular) followed: *Octandre* was premiered in 1924, *Intégrales*

1 Note to Odile Vivier; quoted in Ouellette, *op. cit.*, p. 56.

2 Quoted in Louise Varèse, *op. cit.*, p. 193.

3 *New York Herald*, 11 March 1923; quoted in Louise Varèse, *op. cit.*, p. 193.

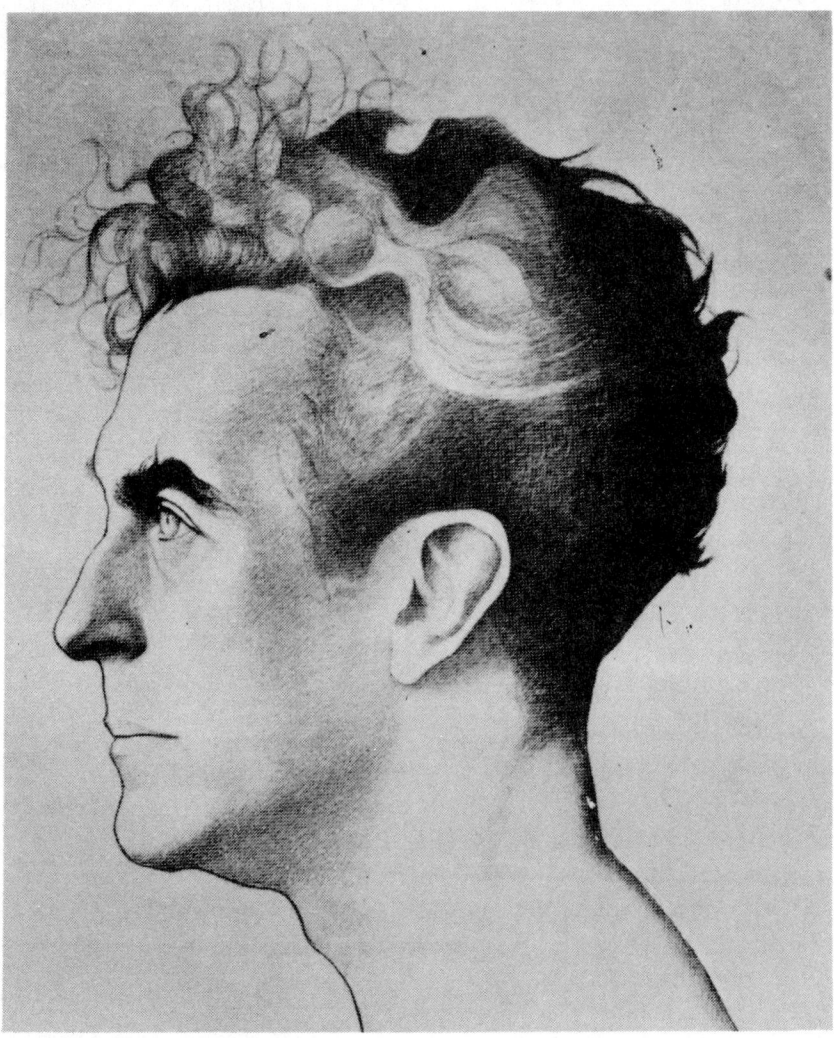

Joseph Stella, silverpoint drawing of Varèse

(for chamber ensemble and four percussionists) in 1925 and *Arcana*, an orchestral work, in 1927. *Amériques* was first performed (by Stokowski) in 1926, and again there was a scandal:

> The outbreak, moderate at first, swelled gradually to an indescribable turmoil. Some men wildly waved their arms and one was seen to raise both hands high above his head with both thumbs turned down, the death sign of the Roman amphitheatre . . .[1]

Varèse's works of the 1920s, after *Amériques* at least, become tougher in sound and more complex in rhythm and texture. Speaking to Schuller, Varèse said of them:

> I believe they reflect a greater refinement of my earlier compositions. I also became increasingly interested in internal rhythmic and metrical relationships . . . I was also interested in the sonorous aspects of percussion as structural, architectonic elements.[2]

The last characteristic mentioned by Varèse reached its ultimate development in *Ionisation* (composed 1929–31, first performed 1933) which is written entirely for percussion.

---

1   *The Sun*, 14 April 1926; quoted in Ouellette, *op. cit.*, pp. 88–89.

2   Schuller, *op. cit.*, p. 35.

9.4   Later works

> I no longer wish to compose for the old instruments played by men, and I am
> handicapped by a lack of adequate electrical instruments for which I conceive
> my music.[1]

From the early 1930s Varèse devoted an increasing amount of his time to campaigning
for the development of electronic instruments. He lectured, applied for research
grants, badgered industrial companies, but to no avail. These efforts, and the
frustrations to which they gave rise, resulted in a period of creative silence from 1936,
when he wrote *Density 21.5* for solo flute, to 1950, when he began work on *Déserts*.
There *was* a project on his mind — to be called *Espace* — but with the exception of
sketches, all destroyed, and a short (and unpublished) *Etude pour Espace* (1947) this
was never realized. Varèse's 'programme' for *Espace* gave as its theme 'TODAY. The
world awakes! Humanity on the march. Nothing can stop it.', and spoke of

> Voices in the sky, as though magic, invisible hands were turning on and off the
> knob of fantastic radios, filling all space, criss-crossing, overlapping,
> penetrating each other, splitting up, superimposing, repulsing each other,
> colliding, crashing.[2]

He envisaged performances being broadcast simultaneously in and from all the
capitals of the world. Choirs in each city would take part; all men could listen. One is
reminded unavoidably of Ives' *Universe Symphony*, also unrealized.

With the development of magnetic tape and the electronic studio after the Second
World War, Varèse resumed composition. *Déserts* uses both orchestral and taped
sound. Two other works are purely electronic: *Poéme Electronique* was produced for
the Brussels World Fair of 1958 and was staged in a building designed by Le Corbusier
for the Philips company as part of a sound and light spectacle; *La Procession de
Verges* was a film soundtrack. There was no historical demarcation between old and
new resources in Varèse's mind, however: his last pieces, *Nocturnal* and the unfinished
Nuits, return to traditional instruments and the voice. He died on 6 November 1965.

Varèse's work table at the time of his death in 1965

1   Letter from Varèse to Léon Theremin (inventor of an electronic instrument named after him), 5 May
1941; quoted in Ouellette, *op. cit.*, p. 128.

2   *Twice a year*, No. 7 (Autumn-Winter 1941); quoted in Ouellette, *op. cit.*, p. 131.

10 Ideas and attitudes

10.1 The composer

As you can see, Varèse was a radical experimenter. He was vehemently opposed to conservative forces within the musical world, to those who 'lie down in other men's thoughts' (Romain Rolland). His conception of the composer's role is described in a lecture he gave in 1939, an extract from which appears in the *Documents* (pp. 69–70).

EXERCISE

Read extract 22. What are the tenets that underlie Varèse's view of the composer's function?

DISCUSSION

1 He should 'express himself and his epoch'.
2 'The very basis of creative work is experimentation.'
3 All great composers in the past were revolutionaries.
4 'It is the artist who crystallizes his age.'
5 The needs of *this* age are for 'music as an art-science' — the new possibilities of sound created by electronic machines.

Not surprisingly Varèse was against Neoclassicism — though not uninterested in the music of the past, as you can see from the first paragraph of extract 23 in the *Documents* (p. 70). 'What is called neo-classicism', he wrote,

> is really academicism . . . it stifles spontaneous expression . . . it is lassitude constructing a theory by which to excuse itself . . . It is perhaps normal at a time of world-wide hesitancy to wish to escape into the categorical past, but life with its exigencies goes on and in the end will sweep away all that is static, all that does not move with the rhythm of life itself . . .[1]

He was unhappy that so many young American composers in the 1920s went to Europe to study, particularly to the celebrated teacher Nadia Boulanger in Paris. 'American music must speak its own language, and not be the result of a certain mummified European formula.'[2] He admired Schoenberg but hated the twelve-note method, along with all other systems. In the ICG Manifesto he declared that he 'disapproves of all "isms"; denies the existence of schools; recognizes only the individual.'

10.2 The music

EXERCISE

If you have not already done so, listen to Octandre *(Record 8, side 2 bands 5 and 6), preferably two or three times, without looking at the extract from the score included in* Scores 7. Try to decide which elements of musical language (rhythm, melody, timbre, etc.) are important and which not important. Write down a few adjectives describing the nature of Varèse's treatment of the important elements.

---

1 Quoted in Ouellette, *op. cit.*, pp. 114, 125.
2 Quoted in Ouellette, *op. cit.*, p. 113.

DISCUSSION

Harmony and melody in the traditional sense are of negligible importance. There are no conventional chords: vertical aggregations of pitches may be described in terms of texture, as much as in terms of harmony. There are few melodic phrases of more than two or three notes. On the other hand, rhythm is immensely important; typically the patterns are highly varied, complex and irregular. Timbre and dynamics are prominent elements too, and again they are very varied — also often harsh, strident and extreme. Texture plays an important part in articulating the form. No traditional forms are followed; instead there is a succession of blocks, each of which works on and varies brief musical ideas ('sound masses', to use Varèse's term). These are presented in juxtaposition and superimposition. Multi-layered effects in which different textures are crossing, overlapping and counterpointing each other, are common.

Harmony

The American composer Henry Cowell has remarked that Varèse does not break any of the rules of ordinary harmony, but that those rules do not even enter into consideration, since they are not pertinent to the different art at which Varèse is aiming. 'One key to a comprehension of Varèse's music', Cowell continues, 'is the fact that he is more interested in finding a note that will sound a certain way in a certain instrument and will "sound" in the orchestral fabric than he is in just what position the note occupies in the harmony, except of course, in so far as its harmonic position will pertain to its "coming out" in the scoring.

'One must consider that besides the harmony of notes, which with Varèse is somewhat secondary, there is at any given time also a harmony of tone-qualities, each of which is calculated to sound out through the orchestra. For example, Varèse will use a certain chord. Superimposed upon this chord and more important than the chord itself to Varèse, is the harmony resultant from the tone-qualities of the instruments owing to their particular sound in the register in which he scores each; so that, while the chord might be found in many a modern composer's work, it assumes a character found only in Varèse when we see it in his particular scoring.' Shortly after Varèse's death, André Jolivet wrote: 'At all events, if we take Hindemith as our reference (in his *Treatise on Harmony*), then Schoenberg's works are still faithful to the traditional harmonic functions of sub-dominant, dominant, and tonic. Varèse, on the other hand, arrived at a point on this syntactical level where he truly succeeded in dominating tonality (so as to exclude it) to an extent that produces effects of detemperization'. Gilles Tremblay, a Canadian composer, has this to say: 'One of Varèse's principal contributions is to have broadened the scope of harmony . . . by restoring it to its primitive role as resonance and timbre.' Lastly, François Morel, another Canadian composer, adds: 'Varèse looks upon chords as objects, as bodies of sound similar to superimpositions of frequencies and not as vertical coagulations above the harmonic functions proper.'[1]

Pitch

Henry Cowell writes that 'one finds that dynamic nuances on the same note, or repeated tones, often take the place of melody. He very frequently does away with melody entirely by having only repeated tones for certain passages. Removing from the listener's ear that which it is accustomed to follow most closely, sometimes almost to the exclusion of everything else, naturally induces a keener awareness of other musical elements such as rhythm and dynamics.

---

1 Ouellette, *op. cit.*, p. 59.

Varèse, however, is always careful to supply the ear with subtleties of dynamic change which take the place of melody in certain passages.' Analyzing Varèse's use of melody, François Morel described it thus: 'The phrase, generally composed of disjunct or linked notes, moves constantly from one register to the other and allows itself to be attracted by the magnetic force of these "pivot-notes," (kinds of dominants) either changing its timbre and color, or not, by means of differing instrumentations . . .' Gilles Tremblay writes: 'When the body of sound thins down till it is monody, the musical fabric, as though relieved of a burden, springs to life and becomes melodic. This is perhaps a transmutation of the vertical into the horizontal, to use one of the terms of alchemy . . .'[1]

But if melody is all but done away with, this does not mean that Varèse's ideas for the area of pitch relationships were not adventurous and of rich implications.

He liked to work with 'pitch areas', characterized by a certain intervallic content: two notes a semitone apart would be a simple example. Used vertically and horizontally, backwards, at different pitches, at different registers, with different timbres, in different rhythms, this could become the basis of the 'sound masses'. Such materials replace conventional themes and tonalities, though they act in a sense as tonics or at least zones of stability, from which the work as a whole is derived.

Like Busoni (and Ives), Varèse wanted to see a much greater variety of ways of dividing up the pitch spectrum. One major disagreement was over the matter of tuning scales and intervals. In the sixth century BC, Pythagoras, by experiment and calculation, had shown that the interval of an *exact* perfect fifth was an interval suited to form the basis of a scalar system. In theory, this looks quite workable: if enough fifths are piled up on each other every one of the twelve possible semitones will be included, as the diagram shows:

C G D A E B F sharp C sharp G sharp D sharp A sharp E sharp
  B sharp (C)

In practice, however, if all of these fifths are perfect, the two Cs (at the bottom and at the top of this compilation) will not be in tune. They will disagree with each other since the upper note will be sharper than the lower, and this disagreement ('out-of-tune-ness') is known as the Pythagorean comma. If an instrument is to be able to play eighteenth- and nineteenth-century tonal music written in any key this disagreement must be removed so that all notes of the same letter name and their enharmonic equivalents are exactly in tune with each other. This means that each of these Pythagorean fifths must be very slightly flattened (or 'tempered', hence the term tempered tuning) in order that the Pythagorean comma may be gradually absorbed. If all notes are slightly and evenly out of tune this tonal problem will pass unnoticed.

Varèse, however, disagreed violently with this process. While the nineteenth century had generally regarded the notes D sharp and E flat (or B sharp and C) as identical (enharmonic equivalents) he claimed that they were two quite distinct and separate sounds which had been distorted by tempered tuning until they had lost their individual identities. If this individuality were to be restored, then the above chart could be extended. The number of single notes available to a composer would not be merely an ascending repeated cycle of twelve notes but an unending and unrepeating succession. The diagram would therefore have to begin as follows, without any enharmonic changes:

C G D A E B F sharp C sharp G sharp D sharp A sharp E sharp B sharp
F double sharp C double sharp G double sharp D double sharp A double sharp
E double sharp B double sharp F triple sharp C triple sharp G triple sharp etc.

1 Ouellette, *op. cit.*, pp. 59–60.

As can be seen from this chart, there are no octaves (because we must not assume that B sharp and C are the same note). It therefore follows that, in Varèse's theory, octave transpositions and doublings—regular features of previous musical styles—are quite impossible. So too is modulation in the traditional sense, and so is the twelve-note method. These depend on tempered tuning and so, like octave transposition, represent merely a form of distortion. Of course the application of such a theory using conventional instruments is largely impractical, but electronic instruments would make it a possibility.

Timbre, intensities, orchestration, rhythm

As for timbre: 'Whereas the Romantic orchestra, with Berlioz and Wagner, was aiming at a fusion of timbres,' Odile Vivier writes, 'for Varèse, on the contrary, timbre has to create the differentiation between waves, levels, and volumes; one could compare it to the line and the play of light which give certain drawings the precision and perspective of space.'

Rhythms and intensities are another concept. Stravinsky has said, in conversation with Robert Craft: 'Varèse was also one of the first composers to employ dynamics as an integral formal element . . . and he was also among the first to plot the intensities of a composition, the highs and lows in pitch, speed, density, rhythmic movement.'

As Gilles Tremblay insists: 'The essential role of rhythm and *dynamics* (intensity) will be to model the sound, to surround it in all its dimensions and to sculpt it . . . Thus we may say that durations give sound its dimension in time, whereas dynamics shape its volume. Here, the rhythm of the music is created by the combination of the two and is centered on the formation of the sound, since in Varèse's work it is the sound which is master of everything else.'[1]

Speaking of orchestration, Varèse has said: 'To me, orchestration is an essential part of the structure of a work. Timbres and their combination—or better, quality of tones and tone-compounds of different pitch, instead of being incidental, become part of the form, coloring and making discernible the different planes and various sound-masses, and so creating the sensation of non-blending. Variations in the intensity of certain tones of the compounds modify the structure of the masses and planes. Contrasting dynamics are based on the play of simultaneously opposing loudnesses—loudness as defined by Harvey Fletcher as "the magnitude of sensation".' Henry Cowell observed on this subject: 'I have frequently noticed that when Varèse examines a new score, he is more interested in the orchestration than in the musical content. . . .'[2]

Unlike the Futurists, however, Varèse was not interested in new sounds and in noises for their own sake. 'The Futurists believe in reproducing sounds literally,' he said. 'I believe in the metamorphosis of sounds into music.'[3]

For Varèse's conception of rhythm see also extract 23 in the *Documents*, paragraph 4. Here he is talking about macro-rhythm (rather than small-scale rhythmic patterns): that is, the durational relationships of events, materials and tensions. Which takes us into the area of form.

Form, texture and sound projection

Read extract 23 in the Documents, *paragraph 4 to the end*. Here Varèse describes form as *process* and uses a favourite analogy—the formation of crystals. For the part to be played in this by texture and what Varèse called 'sound projection', see extract 21, paragraphs 5–8.

1   Ouellette, *op. cit.*, p. 59.
2   Ouellette, *op. cit.*, p. 60.
3   Quoted in Chou Wen-Chung, 'Varèse: A Sketch of the Man and His Music', *Musical Quarterly*, **52**,2 (April 1966).

The operation of 'sound projection' in the case of one specific work—*Intégrales*—is described thus:

> '*Intégrales* was conceived for a spatial projection. I constructed the work to employ certain acoustical means which did not yet exist, but which I knew could be realized and would be used sooner or later . . . Whereas in our musical system we divide up quantities whose values are fixed, in the realization I wanted, the values would have been continually changing in relation to a constant. In other words, it would have been like a series of variations, the changes resulting from slight alterations of a function's form or from the transposition of one function to another. In order to make myself better understood—for the eye is quicker and more disciplined than the ear—let us transfer this conception into the visual sphere and consider the changing projection of a geometrical figure onto a plane surface, with both geometrical figure and plane surface moving in space, but each at its own changing and varying speeds of lateral movement and rotation. The form of the projection at any given instant is determined by the relative orientation of the figure and the surface at that instant. But by allowing both figure and surface to have their own movements, one is able to represent with that projection an apparently unpredictable image of a high degree of complexity; moreover, these qualities can be increased subsequently by permitting the form of the geometrical figure to vary as well as its speeds . . .' It was while listening to the scherzo of Beethoven's Seventh Symphony, one day in the Salle Pleyel in Paris, that Varèse first had the sensation of a 'projection in space.' 'Probably because the hall happened to be over-resonant . . . I became conscious of an entirely new effect produced by this familiar music,' Varèse said. 'I seemed to feel the music detaching itself and projecting itself in space. I became conscious of a third dimension in the music. I call this phenomenon "sound projection", or the feeling given us by certain blocks of sound. Probably I should call them beams of sound, since the feeling is akin to that aroused by beams of light sent forth by a powerful searchlight. For the ear—just as for the eye—it gives a sense of prolongation, a journey into space.'[1]

10.3   The future

Clearly Varèse's conceptions could be only incompletely realized using conventional instruments, and he spent much of his time campaigning for the development of electronic instruments.

EXERCISE

Read extracts 21 and 22 in the Documents *(pp. 68–70).*
1   What reasons are suggested to explain the need for electronic instruments?
2   What will be the capabilities and advantages of the new instruments?

DISCUSSION

1(a) To express a new world.
 (b) To realize Varèse's own conceptions of music.
 (c) Because music is *sound*; new sounds are its lifeblood.
2(a) Differentiation of sound masses, and their projection in space.
 (b) Freedom from the tempered scale, and the opening up and extension of the pitch spectrum.
 (c) New harmonic effects.

1   Ouellette, *op. cit.*, pp. 83–84.

(d) New timbres and an extended dynamic range.

(e) Cross rhythms too complex for human performers.

(f) Freedom from 'interpretation'.

Varèse, however, did not regard electronic instruments as a replacement for conventional ones but as an additional resource — as you can see from extract 23 paragraph 2 in the *Documents*.

In 1913, while still in Europe, Varèse had met René Bertrand, who was working on an electronic instrument called the Dynaphone. Later he met Leo Theremin, a Russian who came to New York, and who made two of his instruments (Theremins) for use in Varèse's *Ecuatorial*. He was also familiar with the Trautonium (invented by Friedrich Trautwein) and the Ondes Martenot (invented by Maurice Martenot). All these instruments produced electronically-generated sound, but only one pitch at a time and of a very limited nature. Further research was urgently needed and Varèse began a campaign for such research (including unsuccessful approaches to the Bell Telephone Company and to the Guggenheim Foundation).

René Bertrand and his dynaphone

Much of this campaign was carried out in the newspapers. In 1916 the New York *Morning Telegraph* quoted Varèse as saying 'Our musical alphabet must be enriched. We also need new instruments very badly.' In the *Christian Science Monitor* in 1922 he elaborated further:

> What we want is an instrument that will give us a continuous sound at any pitch. The composer and the electrician will have to labour together to get it . . . speed and synthesis are characteristics of our own epoch. We need twentieth-century instruments to help us realize them in music.

The battle was even carried into the English press. On 14 June 1924 both the *Daily Mail* and the *Evening News* carried a letter from Varèse in which he stated that 'We need to make a new and simpler approach to music. The development of the art has been hampered by certain mechanical restrictions which no longer need prevail.'

The response to Varèse's campaign was depressing:

> Having been closely associated with scientists of the Bell Laboratories, with Bertrand, inventor of the first electronic instruments, the Dynaphone, and with Theremin, who made two electronic instruments for my *Ecuatorial*, I knew what the possibilities were. I wanted to work with an electrical engineer in a well equipped laboratory. Individual scientists became interested in my idea but their companies did not.[1]

His dream was only to be realized in the 1950s; in the 1920s Varèse had to be content with traditional instruments. If he wished to write his 'new' music it would have to be severely compromised in order to make use of the existing resources. However, while these works *are* compromises and may be regarded as proto-electronic music in some respects, a composer of Varèse's quality could not be satisfied with anything less than fully realized compositions and they have an interest and effect that is well worth attention.

1 Schuller, *op. cit.*, pp. 35–36.

11 *Octandre*

Octandre was written in 1923. In some ways it is one of the more conventional of Varèse's works. It uses no percussion (unusual), it is written for a fairly traditional octet of woodwind and brass plus double bass, and is in more than one movement (rare for Varèse)—in fact, three. However the basic musical techniques are the same as in his other works of the 1920s and in a sense the conventional framework makes it easier to grasp these techniques than does the seemingly more radical presentation of, say, *Ionisation* (written in one continuous movement, for large percussion group and sirens). I would like to use the first and last movements to introduce some of the characteristics of the composer's style, and then to do some more detailed analysis of the second movement, of which you have the score.

Stella's cover painting proposed for the score of Octandre *but not used*

11.1 First movement

Varèse's forms are made up of blocks, each of which explores specific material or materials. This movement is a good example. Here is a plan for you to follow while you listen.

Block	Texture	Material
A(42″)	Melodic (oboe)	Stresses sevenths and tritones but also based on descending scale idea:

B(39″)	Mostly wide-spaced (static) harmony	Sevenths and tritones prominent, melodically and harmonically. Repeated-note figure in flute:

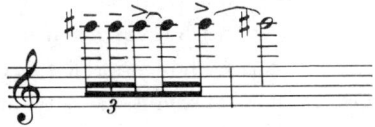

C(10″)	Heavy repeated chords, low register	Another repeated-note figure, in horn:

D(27″)	Varied but on the whole full and wide-spaced, using extreme registers	Descending-scale figure in trumpet, then horn, first against wide-spaced chords, then repeated-note figure in oboe and clarinet.
E(18″)	Melodic (oboe)	Transposed version of opening bars of A.

The 'projection' of sound masses against each other of which Varèse spoke takes place in two dimensions: in superimposition and in juxtaposition. You will probably have noticed that some material appears in different blocks: it is projected forward. The repeated-note figure of D is more or less the same as that in B. The descending-scale figure in D is first heard on clarinet in the middle of A, and is actually derived from the opening oboe phrase.

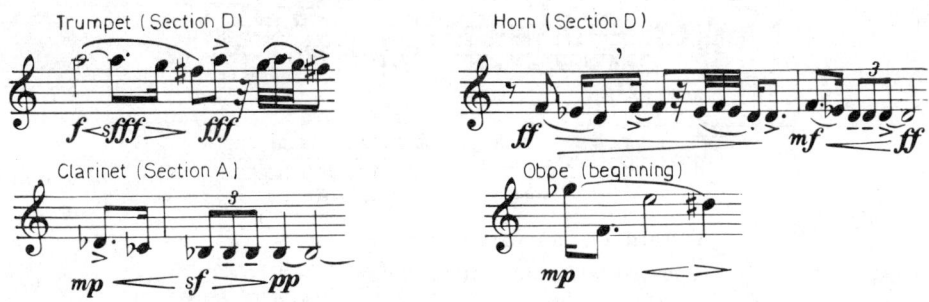

The heavy repeated chords of C reappear towards the end of D in a transposed version.

These ideas are juxtaposed with other material. On the whole there is no attempt to fit them smoothly together; sound masses are differentiated rather than blended. The same applies to superimposition. Block D is a good example here. A diagram of this section would look like this:

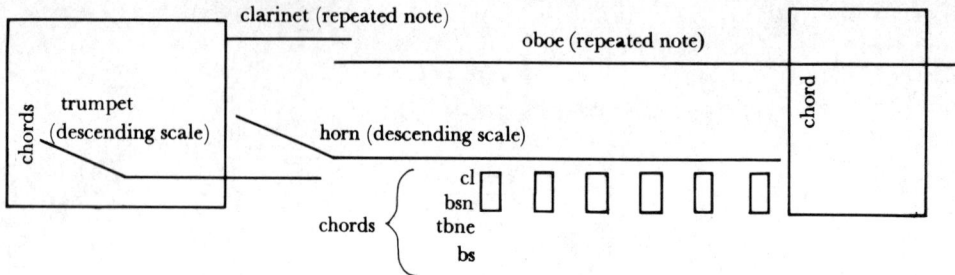

The different ideas *encounter* each other rather than being fitted together. They are separated and differentiated by timbre and register. Notice that through the movement the ideas are very simple: not so much themes, hardly motives, often just a rhythm, a repeated note, a chord. You can see how suitable this conception would be to electronic music, where 'planes' or zones of sound, rather than melodic-harmonic material in the conventional sense, can easily be 'projected' against each other.

11.2   Third movement

EXERCISE

Construct a plan of the block structure similar to the one I gave for the first movement. Concentrate on sorting out where the block divisions come; get as much detail as you can but don't worry if you miss some points that I mention.

DISCUSSION

Block	*Texture*	*Material*
A(29″)	Melodic (bassoon then bass)	Seems to be a new melodic idea.
B(37″)	Fugue (oboe, bassoon, E flat clarinet), then chordal against first bass, then horn	Quite a long theme. Striking closing phrase which stresses seventh.

Towards end appears on horn against repeated-note figure in woodwind.

C(20″)	Solo trumpet against repeated chord, heavily accented, in irregular rhythms, then against same chord, sustained, in regular pulsation, with big crescendo each time.	Descending-scale phrase against repeated chord.

D(11″)	Oboe/bassoon, then all, in close middle-register spacing	New idea
E(39″)	Two planes:1 piccolo/ clarinet,2 horn/trumpet/ trombone. Plus occasional low entries on bass and bassoon	Brass have second part of fugue theme, piccolo and clarinet mainly a repeated-note idea. Ends with beginning of fugue theme on clarinet and oboe against fortissimo chord.

You will recognize some of the material: the descending-scale phrase in C comes from the first movement and the repeated-note figure in E is very similar to those in blocks B and D of the first movement. Again the different ideas are superimposed and juxtaposed, and again timbre, register, intensity and rhythm are used as differentiating elements. At the start of C, for instance, trumpet and the rest are set apart through wildly different rhythms and articulations (smooth against spiky). Then, when the chords become regular, intensity is the most important factor. The recurring crescendo pattern creates a distinct background to the steady intensity-level of the trumpet:

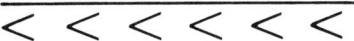

Notice that the crescendos do not provide simply variations in *intensity* but also in the relative strengths of the different timbres making up the chord. As usual in Varèse, harmony, intensity and timbre are indivisible. Notice also that in both parts of this section the rhythmic phrasing of the two planes (trumpet/the rest) differs, and in addition the relationship is always changing. The phrase lengths and the periodicity of repetition vary so that we never hear the same 'rhythmic counterpoint' twice.[1]

---

1 Some dynamic markings are 'compilations' since specific instruments differ slightly in some cases (e.g. *f* instead of *ff*).

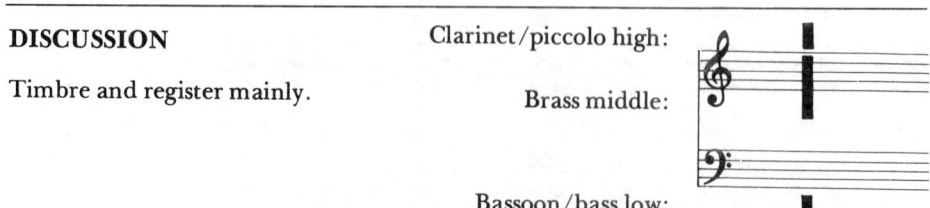

This kind of polyrhythm, formed through varied repetition, is characteristic of Varèse[1] and results in gradations of rhythmic tension. Ultimately, then, we see that *all* the aspects of musical language are involved in the relationships of different zones, planes, or sound masses.

EXERCISE

Block E is a marvellous example of this kind of 'planing'.[2] Can you describe the methods used?

DISCUSSION

Timbre and register mainly.

Clarinet/piccolo high:

Brass middle:

Bassoon/bass low:

1   Though one might also compare it with Stravinsky, notably in *Le Sacre*, which certainly influenced Varèse.

2   A technique which I would not pretend is *unique* to Varèse; you can find examples of similar conceptions in Debussy (e.g. 'Voiles'), Stravinsky (e.g. *Le Sacre*) and the Second Viennese School (e.g. Schoenberg's Five Orchestral Pieces). But I think the technique is more central to and more consistently and radically developed in Varèse.

In a sense the three groups are defining 'sound bands' as much as stating 'musical' material. Rhythm is a factor to some extent too: brass continuous but highly irregular; bassoon and bass occasional sustained interpolations; clarinet and piccolo largely independent though sometimes in rhythmic unison with brass. Actually there is a good example here of what Varèse described as the 'penetration' of one sound mass by another: the degree of rhythmic unison between woodwind and brass gradually increases as the former acquiesce more and more in the patterns of the latter. As a result the brass 'triumph' and the woodwind drop out.

11.3   Second movement

EXERCISE

Listen first of all to the section which runs from the beginning of the second movement up to bar 49, following the score.

How many basic ideas are being used here? What are they?

DISCUSSION

I would say there are two. The first is announced at the outset by the piccolo, and could be split into three elements: 1 the initial chromatic-scale grace notes, 2 the repeated-note pattern and 3 the sustained note.

The second idea consists of the two staccato chords first played by bassoon, trombone and double bass, bar 17 *f*.

Notice that the two ideas are strongly differentiated, the first being linear, sustained, legato, the second short, staccato, vertical. The whole section is constructed out of sound masses formed from these ideas and their interactions. The juxtapositions, superimpositions and transformations, and the relationships and gradations of tension that result, are quite complex for such a short period of music.

The linear idea

At bar 11 the sustained note is opened out (or alternatively the chromatic grace notes verticalized) into a two-note sound mass:

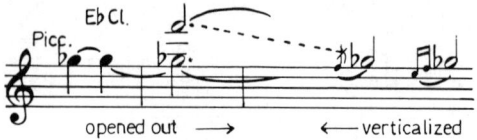

Using the repeated-note pattern as well, this continues as a part of the texture until bar 30. However, from the dynamic markings in piccolo and clarinet, from the lengthening of rhythmic values which takes place at bar 28 and from the lengthening of the silences between entries, you can see that the force of this element is declining. It is, as it were, gradually subdued by other activity going on at the same time. This articulation of tension can be traced back into the unaccompanied piccolo beginning, bars 2–10; there it is chiefly to do with rhythm.

You will see from this simplified version that in these bars tension is gradually increased, then gradually relaxed, by means of alterations in the periodicity of repetitions: first the statements of the idea get progressively shorter and thus closer together, then longer and thus further apart. The placing of the accents makes this clear, especially if we give the first note of each group the accent it would naturally get in performance. The fall in tension represented by bars 7–10 then continues through bars 11–30. Notice that this articulation of tension is created solely by means of changes in rhythm and intensity, not through the conventional techniques of melodic rise and fall or harmonic progression (for example dissonance and resolution).

At bar 17 the initial piccolo idea is taken over in a transposed version by the trombone, then at bar 26 (with a melodic extension down to C sharp) by the horn. At bar 35 it returns to the trombone and this time the C sharp extension provides an upward leap rather than a fall (bars 37–38). This idea, then, runs like a continuous (though rhythmically ever varied) thread through the entire section.

The chordal idea

From bar 17 to bar 35 the linear idea is punctuated by the two-chord idea. Notice that the instrumentation of this idea changes at bar 29 (trombone and horn switching roles). Notice also that the different sound mass played by trumpet, clarinet and oboe, bars 20–35, uses a closely related chord.

re-arranged

EXERCISE

Study the development of these two chordal sound masses from bar 17 to bar 35. Can you describe it? Concentrate on rhythm and intensity.

DISCUSSION

Starting as staccato crotchet chords, both take on characteristics of the *linear* idea (that is, the first main idea of the movement) on which they are superimposed (that is, the repeated-note pattern and its rhythms). So one could say that they take over and reinterpret the role abandoned by the declining piccolo/clarinet 'plane'. At the same time they display overall a progressive increase in rhythmic complexity, a progressive shortening of rhythmic values and a closing up of phrase lengths, thus building up the tension. Within this pattern there is a series of secondary climaxes. Each build-up to a sub-climax 'accompanies' a statement of the trombone/horn 'theme' and it is most easily traced in the dynamic markings:

Bars 17–22	$p \rightarrow mp \rightarrow sff$		29–31	$p \rightarrow sf \rightarrow mp \rightarrow mf$
24–26	$p \rightarrow mf \rightarrow f$		33–35	$mf/f \rightarrow ff \rightarrow f$

This build-up of tension provokes the first harmonic shift of the movement. Up to now the music has been quite static harmonically; the pitches of each sound mass are simply repeated, variation coming solely in the areas of rhythm, timbre and dynamics. But at bar 36 there is a move in pitch areas. The new chord is a cumulation of previous sound masses both in interval content and in rhythm:

cf. Bassoon/Horn/(Trombone)
/Solidus
Bass bars 17-34 and
Trumpet/Clarinet/Oboe
bars 20-35 (see previous
example)

cf. Piccolo/ Clarinet
Bars 11 - 30

Out of this Varèse builds through the next few bars a dense opaque texture using many extreme registers, but ever changing in the precise relationships of different timbres. The final E of the trombone line (bars 46–48) is taken over imperceptibly by the trumpet and leads into the next section at bar 50.

EXERCISE

Bars 38–49 are 'single-texture' (or at least no more than trombone against the rest). Before this, however, the music is 'planed', the different sound masses projected against each other. Can you describe how this operates in bars 1–35? You could do this by means of musical notation or a diagram if you prefer.

DISCUSSION

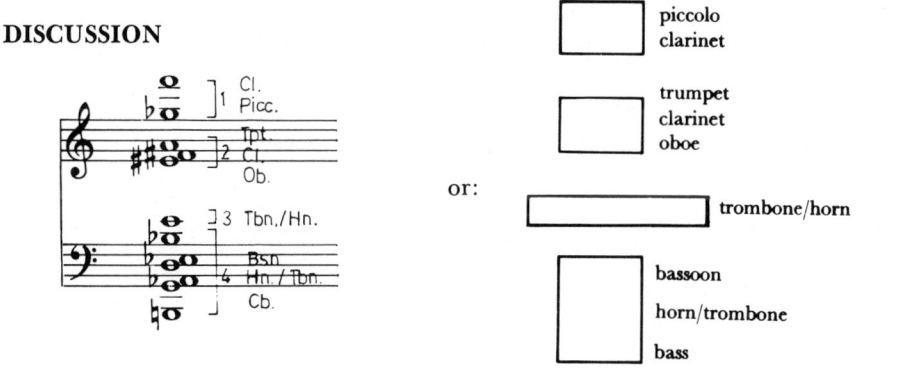

or:

	piccolo clarinet
	trumpet clarinet oboe
	trombone/horn
	bassoon horn/trombone bass

The four planes are quite separate in register—and, as I said before, static in pitch content. Once again we have the impression of 'sound bands' rather than thematic material. Of course, the relationships of the bands in the whole texture are not static but, as we have seen, always changing.

EXERCISE

Now move on to the next section which runs from bar 50 to bar 66. What is the structure of this passage?

DISCUSSION

Two chords are alternated throughout the passage:

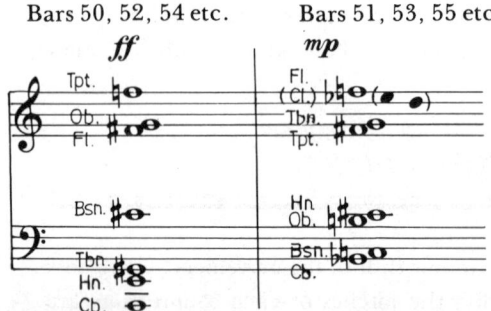

Each is presented in continually changing durations. Over the second the clarinet has a little descending phrase (in many different rhythms). Notice that the two chords are very similar in pitch content; they are distinguished chiefly by intensity (mp/ff), by pitch limits (the first chord quite wide-spaced, the second 'middle-register') and by different placing of the instruments, which results in differing *weights* and overtone structures within the chords. The effect is of 'blocks' of sound something like this:

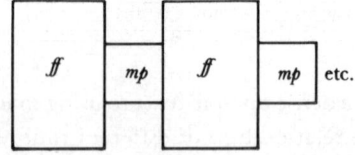

EXERCISE

Obviously rhythm is an important element in this passage. What can you say about it?

DISCUSSION

1   Typically for Varèse, it is irregular. The metre changes continually and the units are often additive (for example, $5/4$, $2\frac{1}{2}/4$).

2   There are close rhythmic similarities between each variation of the little clarinet phrase. Every time—except for the first, which is a close relative—it starts with ♪♩. , and the continuation is always based on repeated quavers. The chord 'behind' the clarinet phrase is always a single sustained note.

3   On the other hand, each statement of the *first* chord is given a different rhythmic articulation. This, then, creates another means of differentiation between the two chords to add to those listed above.

I do not think there is any very precise system governing the rhythmic relationships in this passage, as there is in, say, Stravinsky's first piece for string quartet; Varèse was not a system builder. This does not mean, however, that they are arbitrary. If we write out the duration of the statements of the first chord, they read like this (counting quavers): 8 6 10 8 4 6 4 2. Overall there is a decrease in length (with two secondary expansions on the way to add subtlety to the pattern). Now let's do the same for the second chord: 5 6 5 3 6 7 3 9. This is slightly more complex. The initial five-quaver idea is first expanded by a quaver then repeated (more or less); it is then contracted to three quavers and this is followed by a repeat of the expanded, six-quaver version; this in turn is expanded, to seven quavers, the contracted version is repeated, and then a final expansion, to nine quavers, takes place. A complex set of relationships is set up between repetition, expansion and contraction, though I think there is an overall trend towards expansion (pulled back twice as in the case of the first chord), and this balances the overall contraction pattern set up by this chord.

To sum up this section, we can say that, as in the first section of the movement, harmonic content is virtually static. The relationship of the two sound masses is formed by patterns of rhythm, intensity, timbre and texture.

EXERCISE

What is the function of the final section, bars 66–81? How does it relate to the rest of the movement?

DISCUSSION

It has very much the air of a concluding section, a cadence almost. It moves harmonically rather than being static, and comes to rest on a new and final-sounding chord. After the opening three bars on flute and clarinet/oboe duet (almost a kind of cadenza?) the music is closely related to bars 33–49, both in texture (more or less opaque with many extreme registers and ever-changing timbre relationships) and in rhythmic and melodic content. The initial idea of the movement, in the form evolved by the horn and then trombone at bars 26–41, recurs, again on trombone, at bars 71*ff.*, and its characteristic upward leap (F sharp–F natural here) features prominently through the concluding bars. In its original form this idea reappears on the piccolo in bars 78–81.

We might now modify our view of the block structure of the movement to something like this: A B C B′—though clearly the blocks affect and run into each other (for instance, B grows out of A).

EXERCISE

Why does the final chord sound final? Is it a 'tonic'?

DISCUSSION

It is a classic Varèse spacing:

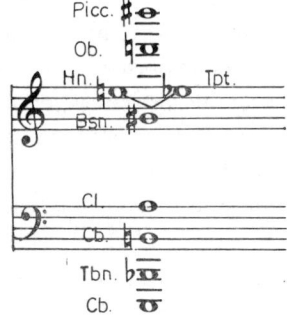

87

wide, covering an immense range (six and a half octaves), full of sevenths and ninths, stressing extreme registers (piccolo, oboe, horn, bassoon high in theirs, clarinet, trombone, bass low in theirs, the latter's bottom string tuned down below its usual E in order to get the low C). The chord's very extremity (of range and instrumental placing) gives it a certain air of finality. But this is allied to an extreme dynamic (*sfff*), repetition, big crescendo and unusual timbres (fluttertonguing). With all those sevenths and ninths about, it is not surprising that no one note predominates sufficiently to be heard as a tonic; but the sound *as an entity* is so emphatic, so strong, that I think it might be considered to have a similar function.

The use of materials other than specific pitches as 'tonics' is one of Varèse's achievements. (In a system which, theoretically, jettisoned the octave this was essential, though his radical harmonic/melodic language and stress on timbre and rhythm made it doubly so.) Listen to bars 50–66 again, for instance. Is a predominant pitch set up here? Not to my ear. But the passage *is* stable. Its reference points are pitch *areas*, intensities and rhythmic relationships. You might try the same exercise with the other two movements, for example the final, three-planed section of the third movement finishing in the whooping repeated brass phrase and concluding dissonant chord.

11.4   *Octandre* as a whole

The use of non-pitch specific tonics is a technique tailor-made for electronic music, which, having the complete pitch spectrum and the whole gamut of 'noise' available, will obviously look for different kinds of reference point from those characteristic of music built out of tempered scales. Much the same is true of Varèse's stress on timbre, texture and rhythm. Again this comes naturally to the electronic composer. You may for instance have heard of 'white noise'; one of the basic resources of electronic music, this denotes the simultaneous production of all frequencies within a certain pitch area. It can be filtered in order to create 'bands' of sound within the total spectrum, to emphasize certain frequencies or frequency relationships and so on. The variables of duration, intensity, and attack and decay can then be easily manipulated. You can see how close in concept this is to Varèse's use of 'sound masses', rather than traditional thematic material, which are 'projected' against each other, often in different pitch planes or 'sound bands', and related or differentiated chiefly by means of timbre, intensity and rhythm.

However, while it is natural to concentrate on Varèse's treatment of *sound*, this does not mean that he was unconcerned with precise pitch. Far from it. The pitch content of *Octandre* is in fact very tightly organized, as Milton Babbitt has shown.[1] The opening four-note phrase (tetrachord) is the germ of the whole work.

It is not a theme, not even a motive. Rather it is a set of intervals (four semitones—which accounts for the plentiful sevenths and ninths throughout the work), a unit of harmonic content, for the notes are used in any order, in retrogression, inversion, melodically and harmonically. In a sense the method is serial, but unlike twelve-note methods it does not give birth to a rigorous system. We have already seen how, within the basic idea, the motive formed from the three most prominent notes (which I shall call X) give rise to the clarinet phrase in section A of the first

1   Milton Babbitt, 'Edgard Varèse: A Few Observations of His Music', *Perspectives of New Music* 4:2 (Spring-Summer 1966). For much of the analysis that follows I am indebted to Babbitt's study.

movement and the trumpet and horn lines in section D (see music example on p. 79 above). We also noticed that the whole idea returns, in a transposed form, at the end of that movement (section E).

At that point notice that the final statement loses its last note and the remaining three notes (henceforth Y), transposed back to their original pitch level and retrograded, then generate the opening idea, on piccolo, of the second movement.

The entries of the clarinet and trombone give us the same three notes in vertical form

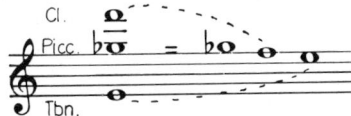

(thus creating a relationship between two of the 'planes' we saw operating in this section), and this 'chord' continues through much of the section (combinations of bassoon, horn and bass taking over the piccolo/clarinet F sharp/F natural in bars 36–37, 43–45, and 47–49). At the same time the trombone itself has Y transposed down a tone; when horn (bar 27) and trombone (bars 37–41) add a C sharp to this, the complete four-note version has reappeared.[1]

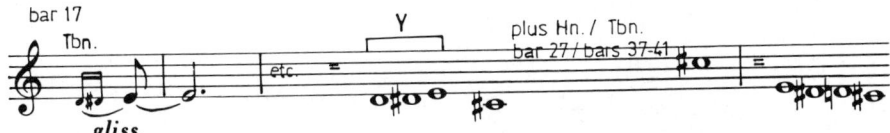

In the second section of the middle movement flute and clarinet between them give us a semi-verticalized form of X, and trumpet and clarinet (which produce the most prominent melodic movement at this point) combine in a linear version.

The final chord of the movement combines two vertical forms of the complete idea, the first at its original pitch, the second transposed to the pitch at which it ended the first movement.

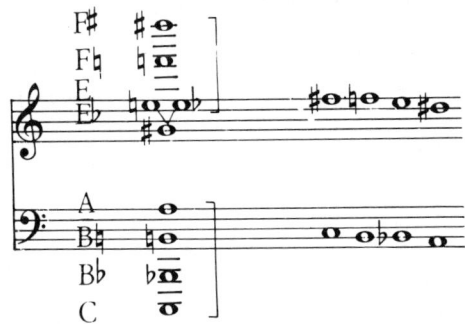

(This is yet another reason why this chord acts as a 'tonic'—see pp. 87–88 above.)

---

1 The trombone line here is an example of how Varèse exploits the potential of the interval structure of the tetrachord for glissandos; his use of grace notes is similar in function. The glissando is one of the few means he had available in pre-electronic days for challenging the hegemony of the tempered scale, for it represents the continuity of the frequency spectrum rather than a series of discrete steps. Another means, employed in some works, is the siren which can also glissando continuously; yet another is unpitched percussion.

The double-bass solo at the beginning of the third movement presents a reordering of the notes of Y at two different pitches.

And the fugue theme is created out of a retrograde of the whole tetrachord, its second phrase then returning to the characteristic ascending major seventh (Z) of the original version at its original pitch.

Section C is dominated by motive X on the trumpet (see music example on pp. 81–82 above), before in section E motive Z returns on the brass, with a version of the whole tetrachord—F F sharp G A flat—superimposed on piccolo and clarinet (see example on p. 83 above). The work ends with a vertical form of motive Y (which you remember was first heard at the beginning of the second movement) at the pitch level presented by the double bass at the opening of the *third* movement.

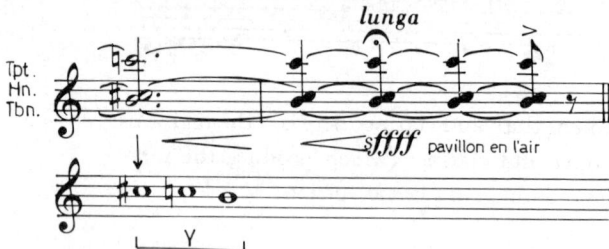

What I hope this mass of details makes clear is not only a further dimension of Varèse's approach to structure—a small abstract unit of a certain pitch content is used to generate many different 'sound masses', which are thus all related but are differentiated by means of timbre, rhythm and so on—but also something of his attitude to tonality. The unit is treated as an overall reference point (a 'tonic'), which can be transposed, thus setting up different pitch areas. Tonal movement and stability are established in terms of relationships between different pitch areas on the one hand and a unity of harmonic content on the other.

12 Density 21.5

To show that Varèse's approach to musical structure was not dependent on striking differentiations of timbre and texture, one has only to turn to *Density 21.5* for solo flute. The principles we have found in *Octandre*, particularly those discussed in the last section, are also operating here, despite the absence of the dimensions of harmony and texture. The piece was written in 1936 for the flautist Georges Barrère's new platinum instrument, the specific gravity of platinum being 21.5. It was the last work to be completed by Varèse until the advent of electronic instruments brought him back to successful composing in the 1950s. *Density 21.5* will be analysed in some detail in Radio programme 15, and the following notes are intended to be used, in conjunction with preliminary listenings to the recording on Record 8, side 2 band 4, as a means of familiarizing yourself with the general nature of the piece.

Listen to it a couple of times to absorb the style, then study the following notes and listen again, with the score (in *Scores 7*). As usual the construction is by blocks. For the most part these are very short; presumably this is because, with no contrasts of texture and few of timbre available, the easiest way to differentiate ideas is by quick juxtapositions. Differentiation is by tempo, rhythm, pitch area, dynamics, phrasing and to some extent timbre.

Block A Bars 1–23 ♩ = 72 Quite lengthy, setting out the material. Basic idea in bars 1–2. Putting it simply for the moment, it is characterized on the one hand by a fall of four semitones (F–C sharp) and a balancing rise of two (F–G), and on the other by the resulting overall tritone shape (C sharp–G) which is split quite prominently into two minor thirds (C sharp–E, E–G). Four versions are presented, starting in bars 1, 9, 15 and 21, on F, D flat, E and B respectively.

Block B Bars 24–28 Change of timbre, attack and rhythmic patterns. Explores C sharp–E minor third. Quiet; low register.

Block C Bars 29–32 ♩ = 60 New rhythm. Transposes opening three notes of idea up a semitone (to G–F sharp–E sharp), reorders them and develops.

Block D Bars 32–36 ♩ = 72 More flowing articulation; high register; *fff*. Rhythmic variations on minor third (F sharp–A).

Block E Bars 36–40 ♩ = 60 Another transposition and reordering of the initial three notes (here E flat–D–D flat). Middle register; sudden dynamic contrasts.

Block F Bars 41–45 ♩ = 72 Initial idea transposed up a semitone.

Block G Bars 46–50 Compare block D.

Block H Bars 50–53 ♩ = 60 Inversion of idea — now *rises* four semitones (A flat–C) and *falls* two (A flat–F sharp). Middle register again with sudden dynamic changes and accents, contrasting with block G.

Block I Bars 53–61 New version of idea at original pitch area, stressing C sharp–E–G; then develops to climactic end. Low register, then up.

13   Ives and Varèse in context

Such reputation as Varèse enjoyed in the 1920s can be attributed in considerable measure to a *succès de scandale*. In the 1930s and 1940s, when he wrote almost nothing and when in any case his music was quite out of sympathy with the prevailing conservatism of the musical scene, his name faded almost completely from public view. His present reputation, like Ives', is the product of recent years. He re-emerged as an important figure partly because of the development of electronic music, in which he took part, and partly because many young composers after the Second World War discovered that his earlier works were of great relevance to the kind of music they were now trying to write. Many went to him for teaching in the 1950s and he also taught in academic contexts, including the famous Internationale Ferienkurse für Neue Musik at Darmstadt. He became something of a father figure to the young avant garde.

Even in the 1920s Varèse's effect and influence were very limited. His music was quite individual and related to no trends of the period. Young American composers at the time were doing very different things. Many—Aaron Copland, Virgil Thomson, Roy Harris, Elliott Carter and others—studied in Paris with Nadia Boulanger, and not surprisingly most of them were influenced by the prevailing spirit of French music: neoclassical, irreverent, economical. Some—Copland, Harris, Thomson and also George Gershwin—were interested in using vernacular American music, from folk tunes to jazz, as a way of trying to create an 'American' music. As Copland put it, 'we wanted to find a music that would speak of universal things in a vernacular of American speech rhythms'[1]. Others were unclassifiably individual, Carl Ruggles producing his dense, contrapuntal, highly dissonant works, Henry Cowell combining naive experimentalism with an interest in all folk and traditional musics, especially celtic and oriental. Ives' isolation during this time was for different reasons from that of Varèse. Nevertheless, it is remarkable to find the two most important composers working in America during the period covered by this course almost devoid of influence until the 1950s and 60s.

EXERCISE

Think back over what you have learned about Ives and Varèse. Can you see any parallels between them, in the areas of (a) their careers, (b) their musical attitudes, innovations and techniques, (c) their influence and positions in twentieth-century musical history?

DISCUSSION

Rather than give you a pat list of suggested links, I would like you now to read a fascinating article written on this subject by an American musicologist, Robert P. Morgan. It is reprinted as an appendix, p. 94. Make notes on his main points and compare them with your own answer to this question.

---

1   Aaron Copland, *Music and Imagination*, Mentor Books 1959, p. 111.

14 List of works by Varèse

Un Grand Sommeil Noir for voice and piano (1906)
Amériques for orchestra (1918–22)
Offrandes for soprano and chamber orchestra (1921)
Hyperprism for nine wind and percussion (1922)
Octandre for chamber group (1923)
Intégrales for eleven wind and percussion (1924)
Arcana for orchestra (1925–27)
Ionisation for percussion ensemble (1930–31)
Ecuatorial for bass voice, brass, piano, organ, two Theremins and percussion (1933–34)
Density 21.5 for flute (1936)
Etude pour Espace for chorus, two pianos and percussion (1947)
Déserts for fourteen wind, piano, percussion and prepared tape (1949–54)
Good Friday Procession in Verges for tape (written for film, *Around and About Joan Miró*) (1956)
Poème Electronique for tapes (1957–58)
Nocturnal for soprano, chorus and small orchestra (1960–61) (completed by Chou Wen-Chung)
Nuits for soprano and chamber ensemble (1965) (unfinished)

Lost works

Trois Pièces for orchestra (?1905)
La Chanson des Jeunes Hommes for orchestra (1905)
Le Prélude à la Fin d'un Jour for orchestra (1905)
Rhapsodie Romane for orchestra (1906)
Bourgogne for orchestra (1907–8)
Gargantua for orchestra (1909) (incomplete)
Mehr Licht for orchestra (?1911)
Les Cycles du Nord for orchestra (?1912)
Oedipus und die Sphynx, opera (1908–14) (incomplete)

Appendix: Robert P. Morgan, 'Rewriting Music History—Second Thoughts on Ives and Varèse'

I

If there is one thing that Western man's recent obsession with historicism should have taught him, it is that each age writes its own history. Certainly in the area of music our view of the historical process seems to undergo more-or-less constant transformation: we are continually changing our minds about which composers are worth talking about, which are worth performing, and even which should be considered as central to the historical development of Western music. Indeed, even our conception of what constitutes the principal line of this development has not remained entirely stable.

Yet there persists a tendency to assume that music history represents a fixed, neatly compartmentalized area that provides us with a common ground of musical understanding. We rely upon it to supply an orderly framework for the great wealth of music to which we are now exposed almost daily (at least for those leading an active musical life). Moreover, we rely upon our conception of music history as a means for understanding the musical present. And since we tend to assume that the present is the child of the past—that its most significant features are realizations of prior implications—we tend to judge it in light of what we take those implications to be. Precisely for this reason, our view of the past holds such important consequences for our understanding of the musical present.

Given what appears to be the currently accepted view of the musical past, however, present-day music must inevitably seem little more than a strange aberration—a sort of musical freak cut off from all precedents. This view of new music may, of course, represent a reasonable account of the contemporary situation, but it raises the question as to whether a revaluation of our historical assumptions would not be in order. And since from the point of view of the present, the most important period in the historical chain is the immediate past, the music of the first half of the twentieth century would seem to be most urgently in need of a fresh consideration.

At this point we might usefully summarize what appears to be the present view of this period: stated somewhat roughly (but I think essentially accurately), it holds that music underwent a major crisis about 1910 as a result of the final disintegration of the tonal system. This led to a period of instability and experimentation in which the most important composers appeared to move in a no-man's land, groping for new compositional procedures through which to form a new stylistic basis for their music. (Significantly, almost all of the stylistic characteristics of this period have been described by musicologists in essentially negative terms, such as 'atonal', 'ametrical', and 'non-melodic'.) After some ten to fifteen years there was then a move toward stabilization: composers began to assume a more traditional approach, either by returning to a new kind of tonality or by establishing a new system (i.e. Schoenberg's twelve-tone system) designed to replace the tonal one, which was considered by these composers to have been exhausted. The most important figures who could be placed neatly into either one side or the other of this picture were Stravinsky, Schoenberg, Bartók, and Berg—and later—and as we shall see, by extension, Webern. (Some would add Prokofiev and Hindemith, both of whom are equally at home in this picture, to the list.)

This view solidified shortly after the Second World War. It thus appeared at a time that was ripe for a fresh appraisal of the music of the first half of the century, an appraisal where one could feel for the first time some sense of historical perspective. The war had made a convenient division which seemed to place the music written before 1940 or so emphatically in the past, and thereby suggested that the music of the 1950s belonged to a new era. There began to appear at this time a number of important books on twentieth-century music which developed the historical view just sketched and which placed the composers previously mentioned at the forefront of musical developments of the first half-century. Further, the music of the 1950s seemed to support this view: its most characteristic feature was a desire for even greater control, epitomized by the development of total serialism, which appeared to represent a logical continuation of the direction established by Schoenberg and the twelve-tone composers. It was the development of total serialism which resolved the question of Webern, who in his works written from the late 1920s until the end of his life had adopted a more rigorous, more completely structural approach to serialism than either of his Viennese colleagues, Schoenberg and Berg. This approach had the initial effect of placing Webern somewhat outside the mainstream, but with the increasing interest among composers in achieving tighter control over the compositional process, there was a corresponding tendency to include Webern among the most significant forerunners. Webern's acceptance, then, might be said to mark a first shift of emphasis in the prevailing picture of the musical past. But it was only that: a shift of emphasis rather than a complete realignment. For Webern's music embodied perhaps more profoundly than that of any of his contemporaries those qualities of formal logic and rationalism so characteristic of the whole neoclassical movement.

Yet today we seem to be at an historical impasse. The music of the past decade or so has brought about developments which, however confusing and contradictory in most regards, have in common the characteristic of seeming to run directly counter to this prevailing philosophy of twentieth-century music. And since this philosophy is still generally held by most of our historians (at least there is very little evidence to the contrary), it is scarcely surprising that recent music remains so totally incomprehensible to them.

This situation raises a real question as to how we should properly conceive of the musical past. It suggests that, rather than considering the present in terms of the past, we might find an answer by going in the reverse direction: a consideration of the musical past in terms of the present. This is not, of course, an altogether new way of thinking: it is undoubtedly the way many musicians (at least among non-historians) tend to think of the past in any case. But it does seem to me that historians have failed to keep abreast of today's rapidly changing musical environment and to evaluate the implications of that environment. Differently stated, I think we have reached a stage where music history needs to be rewritten in the light of recent musical developments—that the past needs to be brought more clearly in line with the musical present.

Rather than assume that recent musical developments are somehow outside of the mainstream of music history, perhaps we should ask whether this mainstream has not been mislocated, at least in regard to twentieth-century music. Was the first half of this century truly characterized by only a brief experimental, pluralistic, and anti-traditional foray into the unknown, followed by a hurried retreat to the comforts of a more traditional and more stable compositional philosophy? Or was there a more prevailing experimental trend which did not lead to capitulation, as it were, but maintained itself consistently throughout the period?

I think such a current is clearly recognizable in the music of Charles Ives and Edgard Varèse. Significantly, both of these composers fall completely outside the accepted view of the period in question. Ives, for example, wrote all of his important works during the 'experimental' period and the years immediately preceding it (roughly 1900–1920): then, for all intents, he stopped composing entirely. On the other hand, none of the music that Varèse wrote during the experimental period has survived, and he completed his first representative composition only in 1921, at the beginning of what is said to be the period of consolidation. Yet his music never reflected the concerns of either the tonal or the twelve-tone neoclassical schools. Varèse rather maintained a seemingly independent position for some fifteen years, when (rather like Ives) he suddenly stopped producing music completely, waiting some twenty years to bring out his next work. This appeared in the 1950s when the prevailing musical climate seemed somewhat more congenial to his ideas: but by that time Varèse had only some ten years left to live, and Ives, who died in 1954, was already a figure of the past.

It is instructive to examine the 'official' position on these two composers. As both were clearly musicians of great originality, it has not been possible for historians of twentieth-century music simply to ignore them; yet since both fell so completely outside of the historical picture being presented, they have been treated as isolated figures outside the musical main-stream—peripheral composers who, though interesting, could be conveniently dismissed as 'experimenters' of limited, local, or individual importance. Thus in William W. Austin's *Music in the 20th Century* (1966), which forms part of the Norton history of music series, certainly the most prestigious series of musico-historical works ever published in the United States (the Austin book received the Otto Kinkeldey Award of the American Musicological Society for the most distinguished work of musicological scholarship published in 1966 by an American), Ives is accorded only some four pages out of a total of over 700, while Varèse receives five. (Stravinsky, on the other hand, receives 61 pages, Schoenberg 56, and Webern 31, while Bartók and Prokofiev both have over 20.). Rather than list further statistics, let it suffice to say that comparable treatment is to be found in other volumes, ranging from such similarly synoptic treatments of the period as H. H. Stuckenschmidt's *Neue Musik* (1951), Karl H. Woerner's *Neue Musik in der Entscheidung* (1956), Claude Samuel's *Panorama de l'Art Musical Contemporain* (1962), and Juan Carlos Paz' *Introduccion a la Musica de Nuestro Tiempo* (1955), to such specialized studies as Theodor W. Adorno's *Philosophie der Neuen Musik* (1948), André Hodeir's *Since Debussy* (1961), and Donald Mitchell's *The Language of Modern Music* (1963).

Recent musical developments suggest, however, that it may well have been Ives and Varèse who represented the true center of twentieth-century music history, a view that this essay will attempt to defend. Obviously, this view is not intended to reflect negatively on the intrinsic quality of the music of those it 'disposes'. Rather, it suggests that from a specifically historical (as opposed to a purely aesthetic) point of view—history being that discipline which has always conceived itself with revealing connections within a temporal framework—these are the two composers who lead most directly to the musical present. Further, it suggests that, at least in the area of music history, a fundamental revaluation of Ives and Varèse and their importance in the full scope of twentieth-century music is long overdue.

I think it would be mistaken, however, to assume that the music historians erred in over-valuating the importance of the 'tonal crisis' in the music of our century. Rather, it seems to me they have suffered from a failure to comprehend the true significance of that crisis. Conservatively oriented, they have preferred to view it in a wholly negative light, as something leading to 'atonal' music—i.e. a music that could not be dealt with in positive terms. They have, as a result, primarily concerned themselves with locating musical developments which led out of this crisis and have failed to consider seriously the possibility of developments which might, in fact, have capitalized upon the loss of tonality. In so doing, they have consequently missed the essential point about both Ives and Varèse: namely, that both composers were able to establish styles which made a virtue of the new musical situation. Their music could not be conceived of as a negation of tonality, for though reflecting the tonal crisis as clearly as any atonal work, it remained tonal in essence; nor could the idea of re-establishing contact with the tradition be applied to their work, which at least in its non-traditional orientation, revealed a consistency notably lacking in, say, Schoenberg and Stravinsky.

What the loss of tonality, at least as a 'system' (and as a system it was as lost to Ives and Varèse as it was to anyone else), opened up to these two composers was an entirely new way of thinking about musical material, and related to this, a new way of conceiving of the nature of musical continuity. Perhaps the most fundamental consequence of this loss resulted from the fact that the basic compositional material had been cut off from any intrinsic sense of mobility. The functional tonal system of the eighteenth and nineteenth centuries had placed the melodic content of a composition in a clear framework within which could be established directed musical motion toward clearly defined goals. Thus the melodic material associated with an 'antecedent' phrase was no longer heard as simple raw material: it was heard as suggesting certain limited kinds of continuation. Put differently, it was given an explicit musical 'meaning'—a context which determined the appropriate kind of continuation. The loss of this more-or-less-agreed-upon meaning clearly had a profound effect upon the way in which composers were able to approach their material, a point which will later be discussed in some detail in reference to specific works by Ives and Varèse. What is most important within the present context, however, is that, of the various 'solutions' offered by different twentieth-century composers to the problem posed by the loss of tonality, those of Ives and Varèse have been most suggestive to composers of the past fifteen years or so.

From the present-day vantage point, the total serialism of the 1950s can be understood as a last phase of neoclassicism: the attempts to find a replacement for the tonal system in a new, analogous system carried to its logical (or as some would say, perhaps not without some justification, 'absurd') conclusion. The compositional tendencies of the late 1950s and the 1960s, then, represent a departure from what had been in essence a long attempt to establish a new 'common practice'. Thus although on the surface recent music seems in many respects more 'traditional' (or at least, as some of our critics have been pointing out, more 'approachable') than that of total serialism, when viewed in a somewhat larger context, it must be said to manifest a really quite 'revolutionary' point of view. What has happened, I think, is that the true modern condition in music is being reflected for the first time with full clarity and on a really wide scale in the music of our own time.

It is ironic that the most systematic attempt to evolve such an approach, total serialism, should itself have been responsible for the realization that the search for a shared system of musical order was fruitless. As has frequently been pointed out, the actual music that resulted from such a completely controlled system more often than not sounded irrational and arbitrary—in fact, completely 'out of control'. Not surprisingly, this had the effect of suggesting to the serial composers themselves that *anything* could happen in their music, a realization which served to loosen up their compositional attitudes considerably. If it was impossible to establish any one common system giving meaningful, consistent results, there was no reason not to make use of entirely different kinds of music, even within a single piece. Certainly the most pervasive hallmark of the new music is its eclecticism: one finds aleatory, tonal, serial, and programmatic elements, for example, all coexisting (and apparently peacefully) in the same work. The problem of unity is no longer solved by a consistent adherence to one compositional approach or even one musical style, but by a consistent attitude towards the use of different approaches and styles. It is just this attitude, whose nature will, I hope, become clearer in the course of this article, that I think ultimately may be taken as representing the most fruitful response to the modern situation in music; and if I am right, it will place Ives and Varèse at the very center of the mainstream of twentieth-century music.

II

It is certainly more than coincidence that everything about Charles Ives—the quality of his life as well as of his music—seems so completely outside the framework of the established picture of twentieth-century music. Although born in 1874 (and thus within the eleven-year span that produced all of the major composers of the period), Ives confined his principal compositional activity to the first twenty years of the century, and nothing whatever (except for a few songs) was written during the period of consolidation. Moreover, he lived outside the established musical profession, deriving his livelihood from the insurance business, while preferring to treat his compositional activities as a more-or-less personal and private affair. It is hardly surprising, then, that most of his contemporaries considered him to be little more than a musical dabbler, and that his music received almost no performances during his lifetime. For this reason he was (and still is) frequently accused of dilettantism, a charge which would certainly hold within the framework of our traditional musical orientation. Viewed in the light of the special conditions of the time, however, his actions take on a somewhat different meaning. Musically considered, Ives chose to be a loner; it was not an unreasonable response to the existing musical conditions.

Ives' own attitude toward his compositions is equally symptomatic. He did not seem to think in terms of completed compositions, and his works consequently have a distinctly 'provisional' quality about them. This is most noticeable in the many small, openly experimental pieces which were apparently never even intended for actual performance, but which Ives undertook as private confrontations with specific compositional problems. But it is also true of his biggest, most important works. Thus Ives himself said of the Second Piano Sonata (the *Concord*), that he thought of it as a kind of work in progress which he would have liked to change whenever he came back to it. (In his own words, 'Everytime I play it, it seems unfinished.') Even the Fourth Symphony, perhaps Ives' greatest work (he himself referred to the last movement as the best thing he had done) was never put down in completely finished form, but had to be assembled from his manuscripts when it finally received its first complete performance some fifty years after its composition. From a traditional point of view, this appears to be unprofessional; yet again, I think this stems from a failure to appreciate the peculiarities of the modern situation, which seems to invite such an 'open-ended' attitude, manifested by a reluctance to commit anything to final form.

Similarly, the accusation often encountered that Ives lacked technical mastery appears to me unfounded. Ives, after all, was trained as a musician from his earliest childhood, receiving his first instruction from his father (who clearly had one of the more original musical minds of his time), and during his high school years he was active as an organist, an activity well suited for the acquisition of a broad musical education. Later Ives majored in music at Yale University, where he studied with Horatio Parker, certainly one of the foremost American composers of the later nineteenth century, and was exposed to what can presumably be taken to have been the best in academic musical instruction available in the United States at the time. He was apparently a perfectly adequate student at Yale, the only complaint being that he refused to be constricted by the limitations of the academic style. (That he, unlike so many of his gifted American contemporaries, chose not to carry on his studies in Europe is simply evidence of his feelings about the decadence of the European musical tradition.) In any case, Ives' supposed lack of technique can not be said to be a matter of his inability to master the tools of his trade: if anything, it was only a matter of his refusal to accept the relevance of these tools for his own artistic purposes, which had nothing whatever to do with a trade. I think there has been a real misunderstanding of Ives in this regard: and I am convinced that a close examination of his scores indicates that he knew precisely what he wanted and knew exactly how to go about realizing his intentions.

Looking over the music, one is amazed at the extent to which Ives anticipated compositional techniques that have occupied composers in recent years. There are, for example, several shorter pieces which experiment with serialism, notably the *Tone Roads No. 1* and *No. 3*, the *Chromatimelodtune*, and *From the Steeples and the Mountains* (all of which predate Schoenberg's earliest serial pieces). Yet significantly, there is in none of these pieces any systematic approach to serialism. In the two *Tone Roads*, for example, the series (there is more than one in each piece) are only one element among many making a contribution to the general pitch organization; and even within the serial voices there is no complete consistency as to the choice of pitches. The series is thus not thought of as the focus of a new musical system; it is simply one among several means of organization. What is even more advanced for the time, the serial idea is not confined to pitch alone, but also determines important rhythmic features in certain of these pieces. Thus in *From the Steeples and the Mountains* there is a rhythmic series in which one finds a gradual reduction of the durational values from minims (eight semiquavers) to dotted quavers (three semiquavers), and then a retrograde of this so that ultimately the long values are reattained. (A similar passage also occurs in the coda of *Across the Pavements*.) But even in Ives' most tightly serial piece, the *Chromatimelodtune*, where the pitch series incorporates all twelve tones and is adhered to with uncharacteristic consistency, there is still a strong tonal orientation. (The pitch C, defined explicitly as a center in the three curious, quintessentially Ivesian cadential passages that punctuate important formal divisions in the piece, is also emphasized through the organization of the series itself: C almost always appears as the first or last note of the set, and further as the only repeated note in the six- and seven-note accompanimental chords which appear in pairs to form twelve-tone 'aggregates'.) Also notable, at least in the context of this somewhat rarified pitch structure, are the eight-measure phrase groups. Yet it is just this apparent inconsistency, both within the pitch structure itself—which is both tonal and twelve-tone—and between the treatment of pitch and rhythm, which to such a large extent accounts for the fascinating aural impression created by the work.

It is in the area of rhythm, however, that Ives can be most innovative and explorative. In *Over the Pavements*, for example, one finds an extraordinary wealth of cross-rhythms placed in juxtaposition to the prevailing (written) meter. At one point these give rise to a gradual acceleration of the beat, resulting in a 'metrical modulation' quite similar in execution to many passages in the works of post-war composers (one thinks particularly of Elliott Carter, although the technique is by no means confined to one composer). (In regard to this piece, as well as to several others, the reader is referred to Gunther Schuller's excellent notes accompanying his recording on Columbia MS-7318 of some of Ives' short chamber works.) There are also several instances in Ives of the simultaneous coordination of two different tempos, such as in the second and last movements of the Fourth Symphony and in 'Putnam's Camp', the second of the *Three Places in New England*.

It is useful to consider such rhythmic complications in relation to another 'prophetic' feature in Ives' work: the textures. These are frequently of a truly staggering complexity, characterized by the dissolution of all details in a total compositional complex in which one perceives only a generalized, overall effect, rather than the individual components. Such passages anticipate what is certainly one of the most characteristic developments in recent music: the emphasis on pure sound and texture, on the quality of the given musical event, at the expense of its relationship to others with which it is associated. (Examples are easy to find: i.e. Stockhausen's group compositions, Xenakis' sound masses and clouds, and the kind of cluster technique associated with Penderecki and Ligeti.) This is most obviously present in such large orchestral works as the Fourth Symphony, *Three Places in New England*, and *The Fourth of July*, where the saturation of the texture with individual elements creates a web of sound from which one is only occasionally able to grasp the specific. Ives had an unusual talent for creating interesting orchestral contexts for such passages. To take one of many possible examples, the beautiful 'transcendental' music in the solo violins and harp which hovers over the last movement of the Fourth Symphony can rarely be heard as a distinct entity, yet it has a profound effect upon the general character of that movement. One of the most poignant aspects of the movement is the way this music occasionally is allowed to emerge from the blurred background to dominate briefly, only then to recede into obscurity once again. But there are also examples in works

for smaller ensembles, such as the Second String Quartet. Even more remarkable is *From the Steeples and the Mountains*, where the notes associated with the accelerating rhythms in the orchestral bells (an instrument already by nature quite indistinct in regard to pitch) are completely absorbed into a mass of sound defined only in its most general outlines.

While on the subject of instrumentation, it is interesting that Ives at a very early date began to show a preference for 'special' ensembles, i.e. groupings of instruments which do not conform to any of the standard ensembles (such as the string quartet and piano trio) inherited from the eighteenth and nineteenth centuries. As early as 1900 or so, for example, Ives became interested in the 'theater orchestra' and wrote many compositions for what are in effect 'pick-up' combinations: e.g. the several chamber music sets and the two *Tone Roads* pieces. Moreover, he also liked to choose combinations especially suited for the unique requirements of particular compositions, as in *From the Steeples and the Mountains* (scored for four sets of bells, trumpet, and trombone) and *The Unanswered Question* (for strings, four flutes and trumpet).

A more general indication of the 'modern' character of Ives' musical thought can be found in his attitude toward the seriousness and exclusiveness of 'classical' music. Ives was certainly no foe of the classics—there is much in both his music and in his prose writings which indicates that he had a firm knowledge of and real affection for the standard literature—but it is also apparent, again in both his music and words, that he objected to the rather sacrosanct aura which he felt surrounded much concert music. Thus he objected to what he considered the over-refined quality of the string-quartet literature and remarked that he would like to write a piece which would make 'those fiddlers get up and do something like men'. (The result was the Second String Quartet.) Further, he repeatedly maintained that he saw no real distinction between different kinds of music—classical, popular, religious, secular, or whatever: and indeed, he did not hesitate to mix sources in composing his own works. Much of his music already evidences that element of self-mockery more commonly associated with Erik Satie, or in our own time with John Cage and his followers, and the kind of directness and unpretentiousness later found in the music of Les Six. This is most apparent in those incidences in which he incorporates well-known popular tunes, such as hymns, marches, or drinking songs, into his music, or where he chooses an instrumental combination with strong popular overtones, as in the theater orchestra pieces. But it also makes itself felt in other, apparently more 'serious' compositions, as in his handling of the four players in the Second String Quartet, where the instruments are treated like proponents in a political argument.

But I have saved for last in this brief listing of precedents for later music, what is certainly the most striking anticipation of recent musical developments in Ives' work: namely, the quotation of known music. As I have already noted, these quotes include a wide range of material, encompassing, for example, the opening motive of Beethoven's Fifth Symphony, the hymn *Martyn* ('Jesus, lover of my soul'), and the patriotic song *The Red, White and Blue*—all of which, significantly, appear in the same work, the *Concord* Sonata. (Ives is also given to quoting his own earlier music.) This is consistent, of course, with Ives' attitude about the universality of music and the common roots of different kinds of music. But it does raise the question of why he chose specifically to *quote* such material, and why he particularly favoured material that would be well-known to a wide range of listeners.

An answer to this question leads us back to problems associated with the collapse of the tonal system, for it seems to me that quotations represented a possible solution to these problems. To the question 'What could form the substance, the basic musical material of a composition, after the underlying basis for the old kind of material—the tonal system—was no longer operational?' there could be only two radical (i.e. not neoclassical) solutions: either one could evolve a new kind of musical material altogether, or one could attempt to find radically new contexts for the old material. It is clearly the latter possibility which Ives explored. (It is no coincidence that this solution has reappeared—along with the other one, to be sure—in the past few years, when the aura of crisis has reasserted itself due to the questions raised by total serialism.) And it seems to me that in developing such contexts he was more successful than any other composer of his time in rethinking the assumptions of traditional musical material. Although Ives, through actual quotation, preserved more of the original character of this material than any of his important contemporaries, he managed to instill it with a completely new musical meaning. I do not think it is too much to say that, whereas the main thrust of compositional activity in the first half of the century was devoted to finding a way of reconciling new compositional 'content' with traditional form, what Ives attempted was to develop a new kind of form for traditional musical content.

Any attempt to understand Ives' quotations must therefore deal with the question of their relationship to the total compositional intent. First, however, it is necessary to return to the question of Ives' technical competence, a question which needs further clarification before the true significance of his quotations can be properly understood. (It is sometimes said that the quotations are themselves symptoms of Ives' inability to deal with purely compositional problems.) I have already discussed Ives' training with an eye toward showing that he had acquired a firm musical foundation. But there is also a portion of Ives' output which reveals a clear and sure handling of compositional procedures within the historical context of his time—thus countering the view that he existed in a sort of musical vacuum. I have in mind works such as the First Symphony and the two piano sonatas, which form strong links with the instrumental tradition of the nineteenth century. Thus the First Symphony, written when Ives was still a student at Yale, is a classic example of an academic, 'school' exercise in traditional musical form. It is not, certainly, a work of profound intrinsic merit (although its many personal touches make it a fascinating study as a stage in the development of Ives' individual musical consciousness): yet considering the age of the composer, it reveals a remarkable sophistication, as well as an impressive technique in handling traditional compositional problems. But it is in the two piano sonatas that one can see the true fruits of this concern with large-scale formal organization. These are, of course, much later works (completed in 1909 and 1915 respectively) and are infinitely more original as personal expressions. Yet both works form clear extensions to the line of great instrumental compositions which leads from Beethoven through Liszt and Mahler. This is heard most immediately in the rich, idiomatic writing for the instrument, but it is also present in more subtle ways, such as in the overall formal construction, which is constantly expanding, built on wave upon wave of climactic motion. Thus the opening of the Second Sonata is obviously 'dualistic' in conception, based on the opposition of two contrasting musical ideas (and thereby showing its debt to the sonata principle); but the whole texture of the piece is so continually developmental that the distinction between the contrasting elements is increasingly broken down during the course of the work. Also reminiscent of nineteenth-century

inclinations is the frequent appearance in these works of a final, texturally rich climactic presentation of the basic melodic material in what Edward T. Cone, in writing about nineteenth-century music, has referred to as a thematic 'apotheosis'. One finds this, for example, in the first and last movements of both sonatas; and also in their slow movements there is what might be called a mirror image of this procedure: a marked simplification of the theme and its accompaniment, resulting in a kind of apotheosis 'in reverse'.

These pieces may appear to constitute exceptions to my point concerning Ives' break with the past. But I think it is necessary to distinguish a 'break' in this sense from a total rupture in which absolutely no factors are carried over into the new music. Certainly the latter is not the case with Ives, who remains in all his works unmistakably a part of the history of Western music. But what is important is the degree to which Ives is able to rethink traditional formal procedures for his own, new purposes.

An instructive example, both in this connection and in relation to the creation of new contexts for quoted material, is the slow, middle movement of the First Piano Sonata. This movement has been described as a theme and variation form constructed on 'What a Friend We Have In Jesus'. If this were literally true, I can well imagine that the results might be disastrous, or at best, an amusing parody in the manner of Ives' own very early (1891) *Variations on America for Organ*, written when the composer was only seventeen years old. But the truth of the matter is that this movement contains neither a theme nor a set of variations, at least in any normal sense. Although Ives does begin, after a very brief 'introduction' (in quotes because it too maintains only the most tenuous relationship to classical models), with a passage derived from the tune in question, the latter is already fragmented, internally altered, and reharmonized almost beyond recognition ('Almost', however, for the tune is incontrovertibly 'there' in some sense), so much so as to raise a real question about whether there is a 'statement' of the tune at all. In any case, Ives has certainly not taken the theme simply as given material and then proceeded to alter it through a set of variations. It is, as noted, varied to begin with, and then, throughout a highly rhapsodic, formally strikingly original movement of constantly developing structure, functions as a kind of periodic 'reference point' for the total musical proceedings. Thus there is no trace of the kind of sectional layout indigenous to the variation form, nor does the theme (or its underlying structure), clothed in different guises and characters, appear as an ever-present central thread which determines the overall formal arrangement of the movement. Yet—and I think this is important—the movement unquestionably owes something to variation form. The 'theme', for example, does play at least an analogous role to the variation theme in that it supplies the general framework of motivic and intervallic consistency which underlies the work. But its actual, recognizable appearances are of an entirely different order; it surfaces only occasionally, always in fragmentary form, creating a recurrent, though elusive, perspective for the myriad of events which swirl around it. (In this connection it resembles the orchestral work *The Housatonic at Stockbridge*.) Further, it appears in its simplest form not at the beginning of the movement but near the end, in the reversed apotheosis mentioned earlier. The effect is thus one of gradual clarification, a procedure reminiscent of that used by Berg in *Lulu*, where in the variations on the *Lautenlied* the tune occurs in its 'original' form *after* the variations. (But the more traditionally oriented Berg is still dealing with a theme, not just a fragment, and with a series of fixed variations.)

I suspect that the main reason critics and analysts have been so prone to accuse Ives of technical incompetence is that they have been looking for the wrong kind of things in his music. It can scarcely be denied that, judged according to traditional criteria, Ives seems at times an awkward composer. The 'naiveté' manifested by portions of even his best pieces—such as the Alcott movement of the *Concord* Sonata and the third, fugal movement of the Fourth Symphony, may understandably raise questions in a mind accustomed to looking for technical and emotional consistency in one work. Yet, in Ives, it is precisely the extreme contrasts created by these and similar movements that mark one of the essential aspects of the music. This is related to the point made earlier concerning Ives' interest in incorporating as many different kinds of 'musics' into his work as possible.

The fugal movement of the Fourth Symphony is interesting in this regard. First, it is undeniably different in both atmosphere and technique from the other three movements, which despite their own important differences have in common a degree of tension and complexity missing from the third (although the first movement might be said to stand as a kind of 'buffer' between the second and fourth on the one hand and the third on the other). Further, it exhibits an internal inconsistency typical of Ives: namely, that a movement couched in the form of a traditional—in some respects an even rather academic—fugue (not even *that* kind of music is to be ruled out *a priori* from Ives' musical world) has as its subject the opening of Lowell Mason's *Missionary Hymn* ('From Greenland's Icy Mountains'). The essential point, typically Ivesian, is the movement's uneasy, though fascinating, balancing of form (or technical means) with content, in which this simple melody is subjected to the most rigorous contrapuntal devices, such as inversion, augmentation, and stretto.

But what is the 'function' of this movement in the symphony as a whole? This question raises issues which are central not only to Ives' own work but to a great deal of more recent music. As the question is phrased (and I have purposely phrased it as an Ives critic would), it presupposes a particular kind of answer—one which would show that the movement reveals relationships, both technical and otherwise, to the symphony as a whole in some way analogous to those found in the great masterpieces of the eighteenth and nineteenth centuries. Yet it seems to me that Ives forces us to ask entirely different kinds of questions if we are to come to a closer understanding of his music. The main point to be grasped is that Ives' work should not be taken as presenting final solutions to musical problems in the way that, say, Beethoven's *Eroica* Symphony does; it presents only suggested, temporary, and provisional solutions. Further—and I think we are only now beginning to see this clearly—this is true not because Ives lacked the technical means to find completely consistent solutions to the musical problems which he confronted, but rather because he no longer believed that such unambiguous solutions continued to be artistically meaningful. It is just Ives' realization of this—indeed his finding virtue in it—which makes his music so suggestive to the modern ear. I have already spoken of Ives' own conscious realization of this provisional, open-ended quality in his music. Significantly, this was something for which he never felt a need to apologize—which, indeed, he did not take to be 'problematic' at all. This attitude is by no means unique to him. It is a strain running through all the arts in this century, and it is characteristic of some of the century's most focal works. (I need mention only Joyce's *Finnegans Wake*, which shares with Ives not only this open-ended quality but also its complex manipulation of extremely diverse materials.)

Returning to the Fourth Symphony: despite its provisional quality, there is certainly a kind of logic embedded in the work. Indeed, if there were not at least some 'sense of sense', I doubt that one could be so moved by it. But its logic is of a different order from the kind to which we are accustomed. This brings me back to Ives' use of quotation, which is closely tied to this question. There has been a realization in recent years that Ives is not just quoting 'for the fun of it' (although I would maintain that this is certainly *one* important side of it), but that he orders his quote so as to establish certain structural relationships in his work. (See particularly the article 'Charles Ives' Quotations: Manner or Substance' by Dennis Marshall in the Spring-Summer 1968 issue of *Perspectives of New Music*.) The Fourth Symphony is an excellent example of this, for it quotes from an astonishing variety of sources. (Those interested in specifics are referred to John Kirkpatrick's preface to the published score.) These vary widely, not only in genre (popular, folk, sacred, etc.), but also in character; and they make the piece appear, at least on casual hearing, to be little more than a musical hodge-podge or collage, a collection of artifacts drawn from the well of Ives' musical memory. Yet virtually all of these tunes share a structural association of considerable importance: they contain phrases which play on the relationship between the fifth and sixth degree of the diatonic major scale, a relationship which dominates each of the four movements of the symphony. Briefly, it must suffice here to point out that he 'rewrites' the ending of the hymn 'Watchman, Tell Us of the Night', which forms the nucleus of the first movement, so that it is not only 'left hanging' at the close of the movement, but also serves to confirm this relationship (the way in which Ives manages to make equivocal the answer to the question framed by the opening lines of the hymn is itself a revealing study); that this interval and its derivatives play an important role in both the second and third movements; and that it completely dominates the coda of the last movement (like the first, ambiguous in its ending—or, one wants to say, its lack thereof,) which is based on yet another tune, *Bethany*. Thus the work can be said to hang together in *some* sense, although to over-emphasize this fact by minimizing the importance of the violent contrasts is, I think, to misread, and even do an injustice, to the piece. For the contrasts—or let me just say it—the *contradictions* inherent in the composition are as important a part of it as are its logical connections. Thus although there is decidedly a kind of consistency in the work, it is nevertheless only a 'kind of' consistency, and one which leaves open as many questions as it answers. It is as if Ives is saying 'Look, even these disparate musical elements have a relationship with one another'. But it is nevertheless fundamental to the sense of the symphony that they are *disparate* elements.

As for the fugue itself, there is a further aspect to the movement which should be mentioned. This is the extraordinary fact that it was taken virtually intact from another, much earlier composition by Ives, the First String Quartet of 1896 (in which it serves as the opening movement). One could say, with some justification, that it has been borrowed from another musical world, relocated like an alien into a totally new and different context. Again, those traditionally-oriented may well wonder how this could possibly work. Surely there exists no comparable situation in all the masterpieces of the eighteenth and nineteenth centuries. It is as if Beethoven had inserted a movement from an early piano sonata into the Ninth Symphony, or Wagner a scene from *Das Liebesverbot* into *Tristan und Isolde*. Yet it *does* work, and I think for reasons similar to those I was getting at before. Although the few changes that Ives has made in transplanting the fugue tend to strengthen its connections with the rest of the symphony—such as the quote from *Antioch* ('Joy to the World') in the final cadential section, which brings out the inversion of the fifth–sixth relationship—it nevertheless appears to stand there essentially nude among the giants which surround it.

But it too has a place in Ives' musical world, and in our own musical world. It is thus both a part of the piece and not a part of it—or rather, *more* than a part of it. One has the feeling that Ives could, if he wished, find a place for almost *anything* in this symphony. It is, in that sense, an 'all-encompassing' work, and as must be the case where inclusion rather than exclusion is the guideline, there are inevitable 'inconsistencies'. Ives is telling us that these *ought* to be there; they stand in his cluttered musical closet as faithful images of the modern cultural situation.

The quotations, too, can be viewed in the light of this inclusiveness. They seem to lend Ives' work an additional dimension, a dimension leading beyond the confines of any specific composition to the larger domain of our musical memories. Ives' preference for borrowed material that is well-known, laden with associations of both a musical and a purely personal nature, almost guarantees a 'meaningful' response from the listener. Whether or not one likes Ives' music, it is difficult not to be strongly affected by it; for we hear him tampering, as it were, with our musical pasts, a fact which has the effect of drawing us almost as participants to the very core of his works. In this regard, there is undeniably inherent in Ives' choice of material a certain nostalgia for the past, a fact which undoubtedly enhances its appeal for many listeners. Yet this nostalgia is of a fundamentally different kind from that manifested by the neoclassical composers. With Ives there is no attempt to re-establish a sense of traditional order and coherence; if anything, he seems to be interested in disrupting those expectations of order evoked by his material. By placing the familiar in unfamiliar contexts, by dissociating it from its normal framework, Ives makes us acutely aware of the new conditions of twentieth-century life. Yet ultimately one

experiences not so much a sense of regret for what has been lost as one of exhilaration in confrontation with the possibilities unleashed by a new world.

I would like to close this discussion of Ives by mentioning what is perhaps his most striking innovation, a procedure which can serve as a common link for the various stylistic factors that have been considered. I am referring to the simultaneous presentation of two or more seemingly independent events in one composite musical statement, creating layered textures that are frequently of extreme density. (Such passages can be taken to form a sub-group to the more general type of massed textural music discussed earlier.) Perhaps the most famous example is the second movement of the Fourth Symphony, where several different 'musics' undergo independent, yet simultaneous lives throughout the course of the work—interacting with one another yet maintaining their own internal consistency (even to the extent of having their own tempos). Other well-known examples can be found in *The Unanswered Question* and *Three Places in New England*. On the one hand, these passages are simply extreme manifestations of Ives' 'inclusiveness'. Not only can two different kinds of music appear in the same piece, they may appear at the same time. In this way the totality becomes literally a fusion of its parts. More generally, such passages suggest a completely new way of organizing musical continuity, a way which is only now beginning to be explored in full.

Although I would again say that there is a structural sense to such passages (a close analysis could easily show that relationships exist among the various layers), their most striking feature is the fascinating ambiguity which stems from their textural multi-dimensionality. Quotations, new materials, and derivatives which belong somewhere in between all coexist in a shared universe in which each plays its own private role while at the same time influencing and being influenced by all others. There is no one perspective in such music; we are constantly being asked to consider the total picture from as many different points of view as possible.

III

Turning to Varèse after a consideration of Ives, one is struck first, certainly, by what appear to be fundamental differences between the two composers. The externals of Varèse's life, for example, clearly present a very different picture from those of Ives. Born in 1883, some ten years after Ives, his roots were European and cosmopolitan. Furthermore, Varèse was always a 'professional' musician in the strict sense of the word; and, despite years of neglect as a composer, he was actively involved in the musical life of his time throughout the greater part of his career.

Yet there are certain aspects of Varèse's life that, in a curious way, recall Ives. His early training was not in music but in science, a fact which the composer felt to be of considerable importance in shaping his attitudes about composition—much as Ives always insisted upon the relevance of his business activities to his musical interests. Also, despite his European background and the fact that he had already attracted considerable attention as composer and conductor in both France and Germany, Varèse chose at the age of thirty-two to move to the United States, the 'new world,' where, with the exception of short visits to the continent, he remained for the rest of his life, marrying a US citizen, and eventually took out citizenship himself. All of his principal compositions were written in this country and Varèse was thus, like Ives, in a very

real sense an 'American' composer working in an artistic milieu which, despite close ties with Europe, was nevertheless to a significant extent dissociated from the heartland of the Western musical heritage.

It is perhaps possible to overstress the coincidence of this geographical dislocation with a corresponding artistic one in Varèse's music. Yet it is difficult not to be impressed by the fact that the composer's first major representative work—which appeared relatively late in his career (he was almost forty)—was not undertaken until 1920, after he was firmly settled in the United States. Significantly, Varèse chose to call the new work *Amériques*, a title which may be taken as symbolic of an attitude characterizing all the works written from this point: a determination to search for 'new worlds' of musical sound and organization. At first glance, *Amériques* seems to occupy an unexceptional position in the history of twentieth-century music. Scored for a very large orchestra (the original called for some hundred and fifty instruments, but in the revised—and considerably shortened—version of 1929 this was reduced to one hundred and twenty-two), it is at times reminiscent of an earlier epoch-making large orchestral work, Stravinsky's *Sacre du Printemps*—particularly in those sections, such as the closing one, which feature highly repetitive motivic figures of an essentially rhythmic-percussive nature. But such surface similarities should not detract from the profound differences existing between the two works, or from the originality of Varèse's conception.

These differences are most clearly evident in the handling of the musical motive and its development, and more specifically in the relationship of the motive to the underlying metrical framework. In the Stravinsky, the playing off of motive against meter forms an essential aspect of the music: the motive, which, to begin with, carries very strong metrical implications, is consistently modified so as to affect the larger groupings of the basic pulse, and is thereby placed in a continuously varying metrical context. It is consequently important that the pulse be 'present' (perceivable), and one of the most interesting facets of Stravinsky's score is the way it forces us to hear metrical groupings, while at the same time forcing a constant reinterpretation of what we take to be the basic pattern of these groupings. In most of *Amériques*, on the other hand, the sense of pulse is considerably more tenuous, and the larger metrical groupings, such as the measure, are less emphatically defined. Consequently, one is less inclined to 'count out' the musical material, tending rather to perceive it as a total musical unit.

Also, there are important differences in the orchestration of the two works. Certainly the *Sacre* is one of the most virtuosic orchestral conceptions in music, yet it owes much to the orchestral approach of the late nineteenth century. Specifically, it features the sort of orchestral dissolution of an underlying harmonic fabric in complex instrumental figurations that had become the hallmark of the post-Wagnerian orchestral style, a point which is well illustrated by the opening section of the work. Although the latter, with its characteristic use of the solo bassoon in its highest register, is undeniably a strikingly scored passage, the conception of the first section as a whole—consisting of a gradual expansion of the opening line through the addition of new instrumental layers, leading ultimately to a climax of considerable textural complexity—creates an orchestral (and also formal) framework stemming directly from such nineteenth-century models as the opening of *Das Rheingold*.

This passage is particularly instructive for our purposes, because the first section of *Amériques* seems in some respects so similar. Here too the opening is characterized by a solo woodwind in a 'special' register (the low alto flute), but the method of extending this opening idea is quite different. There is no gradual building to a climax that serves to define the formal limits of the section; rather, the flute motive is presented and then repeated in an almost 'neutral' manner—that is, it undergoes very little internal modification or development. It is, to be sure, occasionally interrupted by statements of different orchestral groups—a procedure which serves to indicate the overall orchestral scope of the work as well as to introduce the basic thematic material of the composition as a whole—but these are not arranged so as to lead to an 'accumulation' of material in any traditional sense. Everything remains separated. What results is a kind of instrumental 'field'—projected by the flute and articulated by the several orchestral interruptions—that remains essentially 'flat' throughout the entire section.

Another notable aspect of *Amériques* is the importance of the percussion section. The use of percussion in orchestral music had, of course, already undergone considerable expansion by 1920. But whereas this had previously consisted mainly of the use of more and more percussion in an essentially traditional way, in *Amériques* the percussion writing takes on a fundamentally new meaning. Traditionally these instruments

(and particularly those of indefinite pitch) had been used almost exclusively for purposes of 'accent'—to help articulate features already inherent in the 'real' voices of the composition, so that the sense, if not the character, of the music could survive without them. But with Varèse, even in this early work, the percussion begin to assume an independent role: they establish a unique and essential component of the total compositional ideas. Put differently, they no longer serve simply to 'double' pitched parts, but delineate independent parts of their own. One notices this most clearly, of course, in those passages in *Amériques* where the percussion are heard alone (that they *are* heard alone is already an indication of a break with tradition); but the principle operates consistently throughout the entire composition.

Despite the many innovations in *Amériques*, however, in the series of works written over the following decade or so only the ideas implicit there reach full fruition. With one exception (the large orchestral piece *Arcana*, written in 1927), all of these compositions are scored for small instrumental combinations (two of them also involve the use of voice). This can be partially explained, perhaps, by the simple practicalities of musical life: it is considerably easier to get performances of pieces calling for small forces. But what is especially remarkable in these works is that not one is written for a standard instrumental combination; rather, each is scored for a special group determined by the requirements of the composition in question. No other major composer of this period so consistently avoided 'normal' performance groups, a fact which reflects one of the most important assumptions of Varèse's approach: that the basic compositional idea is completely inseparable from those instruments which embody it. The choice of instruments has become as much a part of the essential concept of the piece as, for example, its motivic structure or its form.

But it is not only the uniqueness of the ensembles; the choice of specific instruments is also revealing. Most immediately striking is the absence of strings in all but two of these works (*Ecuatorial*, where a full string section is handled in a quite non-traditional manner, serving a basically accompanimental function; and in *Octandre*, where the only string instrument is a single contrabass). Certainly one reason for this exclusion was a purely negative one: the string section had by that time become so closely aligned with the intensely subjective, rhetorical style of late nineteenth- and early twentieth-century romanticism that its avoidance assisted Varèse in establishing a new 'emotional context' for his music. But more important, it seems to me, was the fact that the preferred brass and woodwinds, with their more precise attack characteristics and intonational qualities, were better suited to Varèse's specific intentions, which were principally concerned with short, sharply defined motivic fragments rather than with the long, sustained lines that characterized the preceding era and were so idiomatically suited to the string instruments.

In addition to this favoring of brass and woodwinds, there is an even more pronounced emphasis on the percussion section. I have already noted Varèse's use of percussion in reference to *Amériques*, but the tendency there becomes increasingly developed in the following chamber works. In all but one (*Octandre*, which uses no percussion at all), the percussion section is by far the richest in the ensemble in both number and variety; and in one instance, *Ionisation*, it actually accounts for the entire ensemble. In these works Varèse not only explored the new timbral possibilities opened up by the use of a radically expanded percussion section (significantly, the only part of the orchestra that failed to keep pace with the general expansion

101

and enrichment that occured throughout the nineteenth and early twentieth centuries), but also extended the very 'vocabulary' of percussion writing. By treating the percussion as equal components in the total ensemble, Varèse evolved what amounts to a completely new language for these instruments.

But, as I have already suggested, it is difficult to discuss Varèse's use of percussion—or for that matter, of any instruments—apart from the overall characteristics of his compositional approach. The chamber pieces written between 1921 and 1934 constitute an ideal basis for the extraction of the composer's general stylistic principles, and a consideration of some of the latter will be useful at this point. To begin with, almost every one of these works opens with a short, unaccompanied 'motive' (the term, as we shall see, is not completely applicable) that presents the basic intervallic and rhythmic material of the piece. The most striking aspect of these motives is their highly repetitive structure—repetitive both in the way shorter, submotivic units occur over and over again (with slight alterations) to form the larger statement; and in the constant reappearance of one tone, which through its accented position relative to the others as well as its frequent repetition, tends to dominate, functioning not so much as a 'tonal center' (which suggests too many parallels with traditional tonality), but as a kind of nucleus around which the others are grouped. Most important, this basic melodic material is so unique in sound, so immediately identifiable as coming from Varèse and no other composer (I have discussed the fundamental differences from Stravinsky, the only other composer to use even superficially similar material) as to suggest at once that the means for its continuation and development will be (and indeed, must be) equally unique and unprecedented.

The problem of establishing musical continuity in the context of twentieth-century developments, already discussed in the first part of this article, bears closely on the general question of Varèse's stylistic procedures. I said earlier that what had been most characteristic of the opening material of pieces written in the eighteenth and nineteenth centuries (leaving aside such matters as slow introductions) was that it seemed to contain fairly explicit implications for its continuation. Thus we speak of 'antecedent' phrases which are 'answered'—and thus fulfilled—by 'consequent' phrases. This characteristic is made possible, of course, by (among other things) the tonal system, which supplies a remarkably unambiguous framework for the establishment of musical motion toward *expected* goals. Moreover, it applies as much to the music of Wagner, where the material has become so loaded with possible implications for its continuation that the latter is always uncertain at best, as to Mozart's, where one has a much clearer idea of the specific kind of continuation that may follow. (The reader should understand that I am not suggesting that the listener knows *exactly* what to expect—frequently one's expectations are only very general in nature—or that he is 'disappointed' if the kind of thing expected does not occur. Indeed, being 'surprised' in this specific way—at hearing 'Y' when 'X' is expected—is a common response to this kind of music; but it is *only* because the music has this quality of evoking expectations that the ability to surprise is one of its most salient features.)

As I have also indicated, one of the most pervasive (and most interesting) qualities of post-tonal music has been the attempt of almost all of the major composers to fashion musical material that despite its abnegation of the functional tonal system, *somehow*—usually through some sort of rhythmic and/or tonal analogy with earlier music—preserves this

character of expected continuation. It is just this quality, however, which seems to me to be completely absent in Varèse's music (a point, incidentally, which distinguishes it sharply from that of Ives); his material seems to a large extent free of any specific implications for its continuation. It is, as I noted in a somewhat different context, 'neutral' in character. Thus, for example, the predominating tones—the tonal nuclei—never appear to 'lean' toward other tones, but appear as 'fixed' and 'abstract' entities defined by an absolute value, rather than by their tendency to move toward their neighbors. Not surprisingly, such material had radically different characteristics from that of traditional music—and thus, I would argue, from the music of Varèse's contemporaries. The most general of these is that the material, since it is not suggestive of what is to follow, becomes more important in its *own* right, as an independent sonic event. One speaks frequently of the importance of 'sound as such' in Varèse's music, a phrase that points clearly to his altered temporal orientation: the material's own inherent quality—and not its ultimate temporal 'direction'—has become its essential attribute. Whether we are dealing with such unaccompanied melodic units as those which initiate most of these works, or with the larger, texturally more complex units that characterize later stages of the composition, the material is defined more by its overall character, its total sonic identity, than by individual details. Thus traditional concepts of melodic and harmonic combination and motivic development are less applicable here than such generalized features as instrumentation, density, volume, overall speed, registral distribution, etc. All of these work in conjunction to determine the total effect, what could be called the 'timbre' of the material. And it is the latter which really matters, which accounts for the true substance of the musical idea in Varèse.

Clearly then, such material must be given a very strong profile, a shape that will lend it an unmistakable stamp and indicate its importance in the context of the work as a whole. Thus in Varèse one feels almost as if the material has been 'projected' in time (to use one of his own terms), hurled out by virtue of its own intrinsic character, rather than because of any inherent tendency toward forward (temporal) motion. I wrote 'in time', yet it is just this facet of Varèse's art which I think explains the frequent references one encounters to the 'spatial' character of his work. It is precisely because we are forced to hear the musical assertions on their own terms, not in terms of their temporal implications for what is to follow, that we hear them 'spatially', as being in some curious way 'fixed in time'. It is thus no coincidence that these ideas are frequently characterized more by some kind of registral (spatial) projection—for example, an *upward* (as opposed to forward) movement toward a high note—than by their specific 'motivic' content.

One could go on, and the matter of 'space' is one to which I shall return. But the question to be considered now is: How is one to extend (i.e., compose with) musical material when no specific kind of extension is suggested? (A history of recent compositional developments might well be written on the basis of this question.) Varèse's solution—recalling his predisposition, strengthened by his early technical training, to approach all phenomena in terms of their physical properties—is typically 'corporeal'. In listening to his compositions, one senses that the material is being handled like an *object*, a sort of basic building block which can be extended and developed by adding on other blocks. (It is suggestive in this regard, as well as in respect to the nature of the material itself, that Varèse referred to the units of his music as 'sound masses.)* The form of the piece, then, becomes the result of the relationships evolving out of the combination of these blocks, some of which are closely related, while others are more contrasting in nature.

This represents a fundamentally new way of dealing with musical continuity (although here again, there are certain parallels with Stravinsky, particularly in the pre-neoclassical, 'Russian' works), and one which has had an enormous influence on recent compositional conceptions. Although a consideration of the techniques Varèse evolved for combining these musical units leads us into a largely uncharted area, for which music theory is only just beginning to develop a vocabulary, it is nevertheless possible to give at least a general account of the principles involved. Certainly any discussion must take into consideration two basic types of combination: simultaneous combination, in which two units are superimposed upon one another (thus raising the question of the relationship of quasi-independent components in the total musical complex), and consecutive combination, in which one unit follows another (whereby the mode of progression from one to the next becomes crucial). Ultimately the two types are of course inseparable, for they work in close conjunction with one another in defining the overall sense of the music. It may be helpful, however, briefly to consider them independently.

The problem of dealing with simultaneous groupings led Varèse to the development of what can be termed a new kind of counterpoint, a 'counterpoint of masses' rather than of individual lines. Since he was concerned with materials which, despite some degree of internal development, tended to maintain their overall, global characteristics, it was possible to 'mix' them in such a way that they could maintain their own identity while at the same time contributing to the larger sonorous effect resulting from their combination. Any given mass, taken individually, can thus be said to define a 'plane', and Varèse's 'counterpoint' consists in a manipulation of several of these planes within the total, 'three-dimensional space' of the composition as a whole. The planes are made to interact with one another in various combinations: they may appear separately, overlap, merge into new, 'higher' identities drawn from the combination of two or more masses, etc. Varèse's own terms for these techniques are particularly instructive: he speaks of the 'collision', 'penetration', 'repulsion', and 'transmutation' of sound masses. The terminology is striking, not only for what it tells us about the composer's compositional procedures, but also for its clear indication of the need for a completely new vocabulary in dealing with this kind of music. This need is itself a most telling aspect of the Varèsian 'situation'.

As for the other type of combination, comprising those of a consecutive nature, here it is more difficult to make generalizations without reference to specific works. I have already spoken of the use of repetition, which is the most common technique for extending a musical unit. But I have also indicated that such repetition rarely occurs without some degree of variation. The questions of how much variation and of what kind are, however, closely tied to the individual formal features of a given composition. They are affected, above all, by the constantly changing relationship of one mass to the others. Furthermore, when one considers the relationship of two *different* masses that occur consecutively in the temporal continuum, the situation takes on increasing complexity. Matters of contrast and balance become paramount, as does the degree of association between 'opposing' elements, which may itself undergo transformation during the course of a piece. What can be said, however, is that Varèse had an unerring sense for balancing the discrete units

with which he worked, as well as a highly developed capacity for integrating these units into larger structures that allowed them both to unfold independently and to interact with one another, thereby acquiring new and deeper musical significance.

In this music there is no melody and accompaniment, or even a counterpoint of melodies, for the ear to follow. There is rather a continuous transformation of the total sound, ensuing from Varèse's 'counterpoint of masses.' This interaction of all the elements and, above all, the way it acts upon the pitch structure—bringing into motion something that in itself is 'motionless'—is what lends the music its extraordinary vitality and accounts for the truly revolutionary character of Varèse's art. For if in tonal music the non-pitch elements may be said to serve an articulative function in a structure basically determined by its pitch relationships, in Varèse the pitch elements seem only to help clarify a structure that is essentially 'non-pitched' in nature. We keep hearing the same pitches, yet they never sound the same. They are different, however, not because they themselves change or develop, but because the elements with which they are associated develop. To return to the spatial analogy, it is as if a set of 'fixed' objects is constantly redefined and reinterpreted by the changing relationships of the objects to one another. These seem also to be transformed by changes in the surrounding 'illumination', whereby the percussion plays a particularly important role, producing continuous variations in the light cast upon and reflected by the pitch events. It is, I think, no accident that one speaks so frequently of the 'kaleidoscopic' effect of this music.

One should not close a discussion of the stylistic characteristics of Varèse's principal creative period without at least some mention of *Ionisation*. The fact that this work represented the first serious attempt in Western music to write a piece entirely for percussion instruments (and moreover, almost exclusively for non-pitched percussion: the few pitched instruments are confined to the final section) has set it apart as a special instance even among Varèse's own compositions. But it should be apparent that the techniques we have discussed lend themselves so well to non-pitched as to pitched instruments. Pitch is only one of several important components in the Varèsian 'system', and as I have tried to indicate, there is much to suggest that it may not be so fundamental as others in determining the unique characteristics of his music. If I am right, and these other values—such as timbre, register, and rhythm—can indeed be said to have taken over the main burden of the musical discourse, then there is no reason why a work for percussion alone should appear in any way 'exceptional.' In *Ionisation* it is not a question of Varèse's having 'compensated' for the loss of pitch through the increased timbral variety offered by a greatly extended percussion ensemble: the compositional procedures to be found there correspond quite closely to those of his other works, at least in their general assumptions.

The question of music without pitch leads us finally to the area of electronic music, which unlike instrumental music, has no particular bias for fixed pitches. It is well-known that Varèse, who frequently complained of the 'tyranny of the tempered scale,' was interested in the possibilities of this new medium for his own music as early as the 1920s but was frustrated by the unavailability of adequate electronic instruments. As Varèse himself pointed out, the use of traditional instruments, even in the radically new combinations he favored during this period, seemed inconsistent with the altered syntax of his musical language. The contemporary state of electronics was, however, inadequate to allow for extensive application of the medium; and although Varèse did use two Ondes Martenot, an early electronic instrument, in *Ecuatorial* (composed in 1934), for the most part he had to make do with what was readily available—essentially, those instruments handed down from the past. This continued until about 1935, when Varèse stopped producing music, entering a period of silence which lasted almost twenty years. Certainly his dissatisfaction with existent instruments had a bearing on this; and there were apparently also problems of a personal nature. But a more inclusive explanation may simply be that the general cultural atmosphere of the period was not conducive to Varèse's musical philosophy: to write music consistent with the new conditions imposed upon the composer in the twentieth century. Amid a general tendency to find ties with the past, Varèse was looking for access to the future. It was a sad phase of his life, and one in need of more complete biographical documentation. (One awaits impatiently the appearance of the second volume of his biography, *Varèse: A Looking Glass Diary*, written by his wife Louise. The first volume, published in 1972 by W. W. Norton, is required reading for anyone interested in the composer, but covers only the years up until 1928.) We do know that he was not completely inactive: works were undertaken, but none was concluded.

It was only after the Second World War, when the general cultural picture began to appear somewhat more open, that Varèse ended his silence. One of the principal factors in his return was that more reliable electronic instruments were beginning to be built, and there was also greater general interest among composers, particularly those of the post-war generation, in exploring the possibilities of the medium. Significantly, the first work to appear—*Déserts*, completed in 1954—combined both instrumental and electronic elements, as if Varèse wished to demonstrate once and for all that there was no inherent contradiction between what he had previously done with old instruments and what could be done with the new. The next work, the *Poème Electronique* of 1958, was entirely electronic. But even here what one hears is basically a continuation of earlier concerns.

It is my own feeling that this composition, as well as the electronic portions of *Déserts*, does not rank with Varèse's best work. By this time the composer was almost seventy, and his most innovative years were behind him. It would be too much to expect that at this stage in his life he would be able to familiarize himself with the new techniques of electronic sound and produce music of the quality of the earlier masterpieces (although, by comparison with other electronic efforts from this early period, these works are immediately striking for their considerable interest and vitality).

As for the final works, several were underway in the 1960s, but all remained unfinished at the time of Varèse's death in 1965. Two of these were close enough to completion to be put into performable state by Chou Wen-Chung. Entitled *Nocturnal* and *Nuit*, they are both vocal compositions of unusual beauty and intensity. But they tell us nothing essentially new about their composer; as their titles seem to suggest, the main work had been accomplished.

IV

In a brief essay on Kafka's forerunners, Jorge Luis Borges remarks that 'every writer *creates* his precursors' (his italics). Borges, who has just finished pointing out some common themes in works of such diverse writers as Zeno, Han Yu, Kierkegaard, Browning, Leon Bloy, and Lord Dunsany, notes that although all the writings in question have in common their resemblance to Kafka, their resemblance to each other is not nearly so apparent. In fact, before having read Kafka, he suggests, one could not have seen any close relationship among them at all. As he goes on to note: 'His [Kafka's] work modifies our conception of the past, as it will modify the future.'

I think a similar situation exists in respect to Ives and Varèse: only after having heard the music of the past twenty years or so can we see clearly the strong connections that exist between them. Perhaps some of these have become apparent during the course of the present article, but I would like to summarize by making a few general observations about their similarities.

In writing about Varèse, I had occasion to mention the 'spatial' aspect of his music. Of the many attributes of his style which lend it this quality, the most prominent is perhaps the essentially static pitch structure, which seems to suspend the music in time—and thus to locate it in space. In Ives too, we frequently encounter such passages. The song *Incantation*, for example, reveals virtually no pitch development throughout; and there are sections of longer works—such as the second theme of the first movement of the First Piano Sonata, or the opening of the last movement—which are similarly 'immobile'. In these instances the music depends upon other factors, such as its rhythmic structure or the sheer interest of its sound, to sustain it. This shift of focus, I suspect, led both composers to explore the possibilities of a 'layered' approach to writing music. As we have seen in the works of both, several seemingly independent components are used simultaneously to create textures of uncommon density. The result is a music which seems to be made up of heterogeneous mixtures. It is 'multi-dimensional' music—and, more importantly, each of the dimensions is accorded more-or-less equal weight in the total musical balance. Thus in Ives, as well as in Varèse, there are many passages where the texture cannot be broken down into a main part and a subordinate one: everything coexists on an equal footing.

In this regard, it is interesting to read Ives' comments on the inception of his *Universe Symphony*, an orchestral work of considerable scope which the composer worked on for several years but never completed:

> When we were in Keene Valley, on the plateau . . . I started something that I'd had in mind for some time . . . trying out a parallel way of listening to music, suggested by looking at a view (1) with the eyes toward the sky or tops of the trees, taking in the earth or foreground subjectively—that is, not focussing the eye on it—(2) then looking at the earth and land, and seeing the sky and the top of the foreground subjectively. In other words, giving a musical piece in two parts, but played at the same time—the lower parts (the basses, cellos, tubas, trombones, bassoons, etc.) working out something representing the earth and listening to that primarily—and then the upper parts (strings, upper woodwinds, piano, bells, etc.) reflecting the skies and the Heavens—and that this piece be played twice, first when the listener focusses his ears on the lower or earth music, and the next time on the upper or Heaven music.

Ives' description is typically subjective and personal, yet the musical conception which lies behind it is very close to Varèse. Indeed, the following remarks made by Varèse could almost be taken as a free translation of those by Ives, converted into the (for Varèse more comfortable) language of physical science:

> In order to make myself better understood—for the eye is quicker and more disciplined than the ear—let us transfer this conception into the visual sphere and consider the changing projection of a geometrical figure onto a plane surface, with both geometrical figure and plane surface, moving in space, but each at its own changing and varying aspects of lateral movement and rotation. The form of the projection at any given instant is determined by the relative orientation of the figures and the surface at that instant. But by allowing both figure and surface to have their own movements, one is able to represent with that projection an apparently unpredictable image of a high degree of complexity; moreover, these qualities can be increased subsequently by permitting the form of the geometrical figure to vary as well as its speeds . . .

There are further specific parallels that might be mentioned, such as the fact that both composers experimented with extensions of the twelve-tone tempered scale. There is even a reference made by Ives to a passage in *The Fourth of July*, in which he says that 'the rhythms are used in a kind of chemical order'—reminding us of Varèse's quotation of Paracelsus, the Swiss chemist and alchemist, as an epigraph to *Arcana*. But ultimately their most basic correspondence lies in the nature of their radical responses to the dilemma brought on by the collapse of tonality. Rather than trying to repair the break, they both accepted the conditions of working within a fundamentally different framework of musical orientation. Their individual responses were, of course, completely different. Ives developed new contexts for material which he borrowed from the past, whether through actual quotation or through the invention of similar kinds of material. Varèse chose to invent a new kind of material altogether, creating formal contexts especially designed for its development. Ives' approach can be said to be 'subjective'—an attempt to play with the listener's expectations through the manipulation of musical material that is loaded with connotations: Varèse's approach, conversely, is 'objective'—an attempt to build structures out of 'abstract' material that is devoid of specific musical implica-tions. But both represent fundamentally new ways of looking at the problem of establishing continuity and coherence in the context of the twentieth-century musical situation. This sets them apart from the other major composers of the period, and indicates their analogous position—each a sort of mirror image of the other in post-tonal music.

Finally, a word about the quality of Ives' and Varèse's work. Even if I am right about their central historical position in the first half of the century, the question of the music's intrinsic value remains open. Is it really on the same level as that of, say, Schoenberg and Stravinsky? Any answer must be of course partly subjective. Granting this, it nevertheless appears to me that the question must be approached quite differently in the case of the two composers. With Ives we are dealing, in a sense, with an almost 'limitless' composer—one willing to take on virtually any compositional problem. We have seen this both in the variety of his compositions and in what I have called the 'inclusive' nature of individual works. Obviously with such a composer there will be some degree of unevenness in the quality of his work, and I do not deny that there are many minor pieces by Ives which are of little musical interest. With Varèse, on the other hand, we are dealing with a 'limited' composer—one who wrote very few works and whose compositions were all conceived from an essentially unified point of view. In this sense Varèse is rather like Webern: he is a very 'even' composer, but also a somewhat restricted one. Furthermore, the music of both Ives and Varèse seems to lack that quality of almost 'Beethovenian' struggle which is so marked, for example, in Schoenberg's music. As I have noted elsewhere, one of the most interesting and moving aspects of the latter's twelve-tone works is the intense effort one hears in the attempt to reconcile a new pitch structure with the basic assumptions of a traditional rhythmic and formal approach. This particular kind of tension, so characteristic of our century, is largely absent from the music of both Ives and Varèse.

But I am purposely going to leave the question unanswered. Music history is not, after all, a popularity contest or a system of musical ratings. What really matters is that Ives and Varèse initiated an important line in twentieth-century musical developments, and one which, at the present time at least, seems to be in the ascendancy. That alone would be sufficient reason to grant them our serious consideration and respect. But I hope I have also offered evidence that their music is able to stand on the strength of inherent quality and interest.

Selected bibliography

General

Chase, G. (1966) *America's Music*, McGraw-Hill.

Chase, G. (ed.) (1966) *The American Composer Speaks,* Louisiana State University Press.

Copland, A. (1968) *The New Music 1900–1960*, Norton (first published 1941 as *Our New Music*).

Hitchcock, H. W. (1974) *Music in the United States: A Historical Introduction*, Prentice-Hall.

Mellers, W. (1964) *Music in a New Found Land*, Barrie & Rockcliffe.

Thomson, V. (1962) *American Composers on American Music*, Frederick Ungar (first published 1933).

Ives

Cowell, H. and Cowell, S. (1955) *Charles Ives and His Music*, Oxford University Press.

Hitchcock, H. W. (1977) *Ives*, Oxford University Press.

Hitchcock, H. W. and Perlis, V. (eds) (1977) *Ives Celebration: Papers and Panels of the Charles Ives Centennial Festival Conference*, University of Illinois Press.

Ives, C. (1962) *Essays Before a Sonata and Other Writings*, ed. H. Boatwright, Norton.

Ives, C. (1972) *Memos*, ed. J. Kirkpatrick, Norton.

Kirkpatrick, J. (1960) *A Temporary Mimeographed Catalogue of the Music Manuscripts and Related Materials of Charles Edward Ives*, Yale University.

Perlis, V. (1974) *Charles Ives Remembered: An Oral History*, Yale University Press.

Rossiter, F. (1975) *Charles Ives and His America*, Gollancz.

Varèse

Babbitt, M. (1966) 'Edgard Varèse: A Few Observations of His Music', *Perspectives of New Music*, 4,2.

Chou Wen-Chung (1966) 'Open Rather than Bounded', *Perspectives of New Music*, 5,1.

Chou Wen-Chung (1966) 'A Varèse Chronology', *Perspectives of New Music*, 5,1.

Chou Wen-Chung (1966) 'Varèse: A Sketch of the Man and His Music', *Musical Quarterly*, 52,2.

Ouellette, F. (1973) *Edgard Varèse*, Calder & Boyars.

Schuller, G. (1965) 'Conversation with Varèse', *Perspectives of New Music*, 3,2.

Varèse, L. (1973) *Varèse, A Looking-Glass Diary Vol. 1: 1883–1928*, Davis-Poynter.

Wilkinson, M. (1957) 'An Introduction to the Music of Edgar Varèse', *The Score*, 19.

Acknowledgements

Grateful acknowledgement is made to the following for permission to reproduce material in these units:

Text

C. E. Ives, *Essays Before a Sonata and Other Writings*, ed. H. Boatwright, Calder and Boyars and W. W. Norton and Co. New York 1969; C. E. Ives, *Memos,* ed. J. Kirkpatrick, Calder and Boyars and American Academy and Institute of Arts and Letters, New York 1972. Copyright © 1972 the American Academy and Institute of Arts and Letters; F. Ouellette, *Edgard Varèse,* Calder and Boyars 1973; R. P. Morgan 'Rewriting Music History' in *Musical Newsletter* 1973. Copyright © *Musical Newsletter* 1973.

Illustrations

Pp. 14, 17, 19 and 57 from the John Herrick Jackson Music Library, Yale University; pp. 69, 76 and 79 from Louise Varèse, *Varèse: A Looking-Glass Diary,* vol. 1, Davis-Poynter 1973, reproduced by courtesy of Louise Varèse; p. 70 from Fernand Ouellette, *Edgard Varèse,* Editions Seghers 1966, reproduced by courtesy of the publisher.